Cambridge Elements

Elements in American Politics
edited by
Frances E. Lee
Princeton University

THE ORIGINS AND CONSEQUENCES OF CONGRESSIONAL PARTY ELECTION AGENDAS

Scott R. Meinke
Bucknell University

CAMBRIDGE
UNIVERSITY PRESS

Shaftesbury Road, Cambridge CB2 8EA, United Kingdom

One Liberty Plaza, 20th Floor, New York, NY 10006, USA

477 Williamstown Road, Port Melbourne, VIC 3207, Australia

314–321, 3rd Floor, Plot 3, Splendor Forum, Jasola District Centre,
New Delhi – 110025, India

103 Penang Road, #05–06/07, Visioncrest Commercial, Singapore 238467

Cambridge University Press is part of Cambridge University Press & Assessment,
a department of the University of Cambridge.

We share the University's mission to contribute to society through the pursuit of
education, learning and research at the highest international levels of excellence.

www.cambridge.org
Information on this title: www.cambridge.org/9781009379243

DOI: 10.1017/9781009264860

First published 2023

A catalogue record for this publication is available from the British Library.

ISBN 978-1-009-37924-3 Hardback
ISBN 978-1-009-26488-4 Paperback
ISSN 2515-1606 (online)
ISSN 2515-1592 (print)

Additional resources for this publication at www.cambridge.org/meinke

The Origins and Consequences of Congressional Party Election Agendas

Elements in American Politics

DOI: 10.1017/9781009264860
First published online: February 2023

Scott R. Meinke
Bucknell University

Author for correspondence: Scott R. Meinke, smeinke@bucknell.edu

Abstract: This Element examines congressional party election agendas, asking first how they originate and what priorities within the party they strategically represent and, second, how they shape postelection legislative activity and policymaking. After surveying post-1980 agenda efforts, it focuses on two prominent cases, the Republican Contract with America (1994) and the Democratic New Direction for America (2006). Using archived records and other qualitative evidence, it shows that both agendas were leadership-driven but were developed in lengthy and relatively inclusive processes. Quantifying agenda content, it demonstrates that the parties strategically skewed agenda promises toward select segments of the caucus, as measured in bill introduction priorities, and the promises echoed leadership messaging from speeches and floor motions in the Congress before the election. After winning a majority, both parties shifted the House's legislative activity sharply toward agenda priorities, but the impact on policy outcomes was substantially constrained.

Keywords: party agendas, party platforms, Contract with America, New Direction for America, campaign promises

ISBNs: 9781009379243 (HB), 9781009264884 (PB), 9781009264860 (OC)
ISSNs: 2515-1606 (online), 2515-1592 (print)

Contents

   A further Online Appendix can be accessed at
   www.cambridge.org/meinke

1 Introduction to Congressional Election Agendas

The seismic shifts in American party politics since the 1980s have fundamentally changed congressional elections. What was once an electoral environment dominated by incumbency, local and regional politics, and candidate-centered appeals is now a more nationalized process, defined by perennial close competition for the control of Congress (Abramowitz and Webster 2016; Hopkins 2018; Jacobson 2015). In this context, both Republican and Democratic congressional leaders have turned to election-year issue agendas to define strategic national issue brands for their parties' campaigns.

Such efforts are not themselves a new innovation – earlier attempts date back at least to New-Deal-era Republicans. In the competitive and polarized current context, though, congressional parties have focused much more heavily on partisan messaging, in and out of election cycles (Green 2015; Lee 2016). With nationalized congressional elections and a message-focused party leadership, the parties have more often promoted election-year agendas aggressively, and they have successfully grabbed substantial media attention in some cycles. Since 1980, most serious agenda efforts have come from House minority parties, and minority parties that were out of the White House in midterm years have produced the agendas that have won the most sustained attention. The most famous example is the Republicans' 1994 "Contract with America," a set of ten focused issue priorities that the GOP leadership unveiled in a Capitol steps signing ceremony and promoted through the last six weeks of their successful campaign for a congressional majority. Other prominent examples include the Democratic "New Direction for America" in 2006 (also known as "Six for '06") and the 2010 GOP "Pledge to America."

These agenda-setting attempts have sometimes been dismissed as sloganeering, but I argue that they are an important component of representation and governing in the current Congress. As campaigns turn in a national direction, congressional election agendas represent a set of public issue priorities that, on one hand, reflect strategic leadership decisions about party positioning and, on the other, represent commitments to the public. They also have the potential to influence perceptions of electoral mandates (Peterson et al. 2003) and, in turn, legislative priorities after the election. Normatively speaking, national election agendas may shift representational dynamics, relocating more legislative promise-making and promise-keeping to the congressional party. In the long run, the move toward national party agendas in congressional campaigns could push American politics in the direction of a congressionally centered, responsible-party system (American Political Science Association 1950). This change creates a new tension in the political system, though. The familiar constraints of bicameralism, separation of powers, and continuing district incentives limit the extent to which nationalized congressional agendas can bring about a true party government model of representation (Ranney 1954; Rosenbluth and Shapiro 2018).

To explore these changes and their implications, I examine two sets of research questions. First, where do congressional party election agendas originate, and whose priorities do they strategically advance in the service of collective party goals? Second, how does the House's overall postelection legislative activity reflect the priorities of the electoral agenda after majority control changes, and how successful is the majority in using the agenda to shift policy outcomes in the new Congress?

In answering these questions, I focus in depth on two cases, the 1994 Contract with America and the 2006 New Direction for America. I argue that the party leadership develops agendas with broad participation to achieve buy-in, but the agenda promises are selectively designed to target voting blocs that are strategically important to expanding the party's electoral support. Depending on the congressional party's electoral needs, we should see election agendas that overrepresent the issue priorities of a segment of the party caucus. I also expect to see that the issues the House minority party prioritizes in its elective agenda will be visible in the party's coordinated legislative messaging efforts. Then, after the election, we should observe these priorities in new majority's legislative activity. Following the issue-priority approach that others have used to evaluate follow-through on individual candidates' promises (Sulkin 2011) and presidential party platforms (Fagan 2018), I expect to find increased House committee and floor activity around congressional election priorities after the election. Effects on legislative enactments, and therefore the ability to meet the expectations set by this party-government approach, should be more limited by factors beyond the control of a House majority.

I begin in Section 2 by reviewing the broader sweep of congressional election agenda efforts, particularly in the era that began with the 1980 election, to put the 1994 and 2006 cases fully in context. I then use research on congressional message politics as well as scholarship on party platforms to set up the main empirical expectations of the project, and I explain the mix of quantitative data analysis and qualitative process evidence that informs the remaining sections.

Section 3 centers on the Contract with America, beginning with a detailed discussion of its development based on archival evidence supplemented by secondary sources. This review highlights the role played by House GOP leaders as well as the extensive involvement of rank-and-file members, House candidates, and elements of the outside party network; it also emphasizes the strategic decisions to limit the scope of issues in the agenda. Then, mapping the issues in the agenda onto individual members' bill sponsorship, I show how the Contract distinctly represented the concerns of more conservative incumbents, and how the Contract's issues pervaded the minority party's 1993–94 messaging in speeches and floor motions. I then look forward to the Republican-majority Congresses that followed the 1994 election, and show the shifts in committee activity and floor voting attention that corresponded to Contract topics, and I document Republicans' track record in effecting policy change based on the agenda. Finally, I consider new House Republican agenda decisions once the party was in the majority in the 104th and 105th Congresses. Archival evidence from the Gingrich papers, as well as those of Dick Armey (R-TX) and Tom DeLay (R-TX), reveals a turn inward in agenda development as the party tried to manage simultaneously the expectations for both Contract-style legislative focus and the host of unmet issue demands from members and outside groups.

I consider the Democrats' 2006 New Direction/Six for '06 agenda in Section 4. I use contemporary coverage, archived internet material, as well as limited available leadership archives to review the agenda's development and publicity. Quantitative analysis of member priorities and New Direction content highlights the key strategic differences with the Contract: Democrats in 2006 chose to appeal to swing districts by selecting issues that were priorities of their more vulnerable incumbents. I analyze data not available for 1994 to examine which incumbents were more likely to advertise the agenda in 2006, finding that despite the content, the more liberal and electorally secure Democrats were the members most likely to follow the leadership's encouragement to promote the agenda. Finally, this section presents evidence on the House legislative process and policy outcomes in the 110th Congress (2007–8) and after, revealing patterns similar to those found for the Contract in the 104th Congress.

The concluding section comments on the implications of modern congressional election agendas. I argue that these attempts, as a distinct element of an intense congressional focus on electoral messaging, can be expected to continue and, in turn, to shape representation. The 1994 and 2006 cases show a through line between strategic agenda content, minority-party messaging, and legislative action on agenda promises after the election. At the same time, this dynamic raises a new set of normative problems, and it falls far short of bringing about a form of American responsible party government. Among these is the fact that congressional agendas appear most likely to foreshadow political action – as they did after 1994 and 2006 – under divided government when they are least likely to lead to actual policy outcomes for which the party can be held accountable. Message politics can become more directly fused to substantive legislating through campaign agendas, and party leaders may continue to use agendas in part for that long-range purpose. But the path between election agenda and results is a circuitous one, and only a small portion of the major enactments in these postelection Congresses could be traced back to agenda promises.

2 Understanding Agenda Formation and Effects: Background, Argument, and Methods

2.1 National Agendas in Congressional Campaigns: Background

National party platforms have a long history in American presidential-election politics, dating to the 1830s and 1840s. Congressional party agendas have been less central to electoral politics, and have become a regular feature of American politics only in the current era of close party competition. Even in this recent time period, congressional agendas have varied in political circumstances, in scope, and in the extent to which they have received national attention before and after the election. Here, I discuss some early congressional agenda efforts, and then I describe and classify the parties' election agendas in time from 1980 to the present in order to set the context for further analysis of agenda development and impact.

2.1.1 Early Party Election Agendas

In a period of decentralized, candidate-centered congressional elections (Mayhew 1974), national issue agendas for the congressional parties were rare. The parties did, however, occasionally seek to offer public positions for electoral purposes, particularly as they struggled over major defeats and internal divisions (see Klinkner 1994). In an early example, New-Deal-era Republicans responded to their 1944 losses by moving to define a set of congressional priorities. According to Reinhard (1983, 9–10), Thomas Dewey urged the party toward agenda setting shortly after the 1944 defeat, and Senator Robert Taft (R-OH) eventually led House and Senate GOP to agree on an agenda. The "statement of aims and purposes" was released in late 1945 and endorsed by the Republican National Committee (RNC) (Reinhard 1983, 10).

The 1940s GOP struggled with ideological factions and long-term loss, and the mid-1960s Republican Party faced similar challenges. After the landslide losses of 1964, moderates took control of the RNC and focused the national party on expanding its coalition and building a brand around centrist policy positions (Heersink 2018). "The most significant attempt at this task," in Klinkner's account (1994, 84), "was the Republican Coordinating Committee (RCC)." The RCC emphasized policy development and communication, and it connected party committee leadership with the leaders of the House and Senate GOP (Klinkner 1994, 85–86). The RCC's role was wide-ranging, but it represented the congressional party's effort to communicate clear, national policy messages in the lead up to the 1966 and 1968 elections.

On the other side of the aisle, congressional Democrats deployed a somewhat different mechanism after their 1968 White House loss for national agenda messaging before the 1970 midterms. In late 1969, the Democratic National Committee (DNC) and Democratic congressional leaders began to plan for a prime-time network television program that would emphasize Democratic agenda priorities and draw contrasts with the Nixon Administration. DNC chair Fred Harris (D-OK) wrote to Majority Leader Carl Albert (D-OK) to pitch a plan connected to the 1970 State of the Union and urging that the response "must point toward the 1970 campaign and be built around unifying issues which can broadly appeal to Democrats of all persuasions."[1] The final product, aired a few weeks after the State of the Union and "designed as the opening of the Democratic Congressional campaign of 1970," involved a range of Democratic senators and House members speaking with Americans around the country on issue priorities including the environment, inflation, and education.[2] The Democratic broadcast received mixed reviews at best, but it illustrates a targeted election-year attempt by the congressional party out of the White House to seize the public agenda.[3]

2.1.2 Party Election Agendas since 1980

Coordinated national party messages like these were the exception rather than the rule in the mid-twentieth century, but election-year issue agendas have become more common since about 1980. Parties have varied widely in how actively they have pushed these agendas, and many of the agendas did not break through with the public, receiving only fleeting media attention. Table 1 outlines examples since 1980.[4] I categorize the agendas here according to whether the party held the House[5] majority before the election and whether the White House

---

[1] Fred Harris to Carl Albert, December 11, 1969, Carl Albert Collection, Carl Albert Center, University of Oklahoma, Box 59, Folder 9.

[2] R. W. Apple, Jr., "Democrats Rebuke Nixon in State-of-Union Rebuttal," *New York Times*, February 9, 1970. Transcript of "State of the Nation a Democratic View: A View of the Priorities of the 70's," Carl Albert Collection, Box 59, Folder 9.

[3] David S. Broder, "Democrats Seize the Limelight and Old Wounds Are Reopened," *Washington Post*, February 10, 1970.

[4] The cases in Table 1 were identified using national media searches as well as the minority-party list in Green (2015, 63–65). The table may not be an exhaustive set of cases – even some of the included agendas (such as the 2000 Democrats) received almost no media coverage.

[5] Some agendas involved coordination across the two chambers, but the House party has been the engine of these agenda proposals, as well as of the post-election attempts at follow-through.

Table 1 Congressional election agendas, 1980–present

	House majority preelection	House minority preelection
In White House	None	Republicans 1992 Democrats 1996 *Democrats 1998*[a] Democrats 2000 Republicans 2008 Republicans 2020
Out of White House	*Democrats 1982* Republicans 2016 Democrats 2020	Republicans 1980 *Republicans 1994* *Democrats 2002* Democrats 2004 *Democrats 2006* *Republicans 2010* *Democrats 2018* *Republicans 2022*

[a] Italics indicate midterm election cycles.

was controlled by the party. The table also distinguishes between midterm agendas and agendas offered in presidential years.

Perhaps unsurprisingly, congressional parties have offered agendas most often when they are in the minority and seeking majority status – the incentives for minority-party messaging are strong in the post-1980 period (Green 2015; Lee 2016). More generally, since congressional election agendas are making a prospective case for change, the rhetorical challenge is greater for a party that already holds the congressional majority. There are just three cases of agendas from a House majority party, and all were from parties that did not hold the White House. No parties that controlled both the White House and the House of Representatives put forward a congressional election agenda (or at least none that left any record I have located), an indicator of the presidency centered nature of unified-government party politics and the limited perceived utility of congressional election agendas for parties in control of both branches.

The cases in Table 1 that received the most intense party promotion – and, in turn, the most sustained media attention – are those that *entirely out-of-power parties offered in midterm election cycles*. These include the Republicans' 1994 Contract with America, the Democrats' 2006 New Direction for America, and the Republicans' 2010 Pledge to America. In his discussion of minority-party election agendas, Green (2015, 62) notes that "party unity" around the agenda is an "important variable" in explaining its impact. This motivation for the minority party to coalesce around an electorally strategic agenda is at least in part a function of the political context. The imperative of majority-seeking motivates at least some out-of-power parties in congressionally centered midterm years to pursue election agendas, and the absence of a presidential campaign has allowed these agendas to break through. These conditions, in turn, create the most likely circumstances for agendas to drive representation after the election.[6]

To begin considering these agendas and the contexts that shape them, I offer brief discussion of four different examples from the modern era. These include the precedent-setting agenda offered by out-of-power Republicans in 1980, the agenda formulated by the Democratic House majority in 1982 after major party losses, the presidential-year agenda put forward by minority-party Democrats in 1996, and the minority party midterm agenda that Republicans promoted in 2010.

1980 Republicans

The 1980 election cycle represented the dawn of the modern congressional party election agenda. In that year, congressional Republicans and the Reagan-Bush presidential campaign tried to coordinate around a legislative agenda for the minority party. At the initiative of "junior House Republicans," including Newt Gingrich (R-GA), a "somewhat reluctant Reagan campaign" was convinced to appear on the Capitol steps in September alongside about 150 Republican congressional members and candidates to announce a set of economic policy positions.[7] The *Washington Post* described the event as "a campaign union that has no parallel in modern American politics."[8] Substantively, the "Governing Team Day" announcement focused on tax and spending cuts,

---

[6] It is worth noting, too, the dogs that did not bark – the congressional parties that did not offer agendas, or who put forward some agenda material but made almost no effort to promote it. There are a few examples in out-party midterm years, including Democrats in 2002 and 2018 with midterm agendas that barely registered in the press or campaigns. Parties with midterm advantages, including the 1994 Republicans and 2006 Democrats, have encountered some difference of opinion about whether a positive national issue platform was really strategically preferable to a simpler campaign against the incumbent party. The 2018 Democrats appear to have chosen not to compete for attention with Donald Trump and the divided congressional GOP. Democrats in 2002, facing a decidedly unfavorable environment, seem to have seen little benefit in a national argument, leaving candidates to run localized contests. Both examples highlight a basic choice that has preceded strategic decisions about agenda content and presentation. See Koger, G. (2018). "The Legislative Costs of Campaigning Without an Agenda." *Vox*, September 8. www.vox.com/mischiefs-of-faction/2018/9/8/17832956/democrats-midterms-elections-campaigns.

[7] David S. Broder, "Capitol Steps Theatrical," *Washington Post*, September 10, 1980. Gingrich's involvement is discussed in Continetti (2022, 316), Green and Crouch (2022, 26), and Stid (1996, 6).

[8] Helen Dewar, "GOP Moves to Mesh Presidential, Congressional Campaigns," *Washington Post*, September 13, 1980.

committing the GOP to Kemp-Roth fiscal reforms. Candidate Reagan used his speech at the event to center the congressional-presidential relationship as an issue in the campaign, saying that "Pennsylvania Avenue is not a bridge between two branches of government, but a moat dividing the unresponsive Congressional leadership from a President who is often isolated and unable to fulfill the primary responsibilities of his office. The result has been legislative chaos."[9]

Republicans in 1980 also deployed an issue-focused national advertising campaign against the Democratic congressional majority. Throughout the spring and summer of 1980, Republicans spent millions on ads that directly targeted congressional Democrats on issues like inflation and the energy crisis.[10] One ad featured a clueless actor with an uncanny resemblance to House Speaker Tip O'Neill (D-MA) driving a giant 1970s sedan down the highway, ignoring warnings from a nervous staffer about running out of gas. His car sputters to a stop as the voiceover intones: "Democrats are out of gas. Vote Republican. For a change." With its coordinated agenda and a national advertising blast, the 1980 GOP campaign represented a new turn toward congressional issue platforms that centered a national message.

1982 Democrats

Still smarting from the loss of the White House and Senate in 1980, Democrats in the House undertook a long-term project of developing a detailed agenda before the 1982 midterm elections. Democratic leaders formed a thirty-seven-member Committee on Party Effectiveness that represented the caucus' regional and ideological diversity. This approach was consistent with the participatory strategy that the postreform majority regularly followed (Meinke 2016; Sinclair 1995), and it extended to a series of caucus task forces that formulated issue-specific policy reports, with input from outside experts and advisory committees. According to Democratic Caucus Chair Gillis Long (D-LA), the Committee on Party Effectiveness met at least weekly through the 97th Congress (1981–82) to oversee agenda development.[11]

[9] Martin Tolchin, "Reagan and Others in GOP Vow to be Unified if They Control Congress," *New York Times*, September 16, 1980. Green and Crouch (2022, 31) suggest that the limited impact of the 1980 attempt helped to shape Newt Gingrich's long-term strategy for pursuing a Republican House majority. Also see Lee (2016, 80–81) for discussion of the 1980 strategy as part of the broader rise in national congressional campaign politics.

[10] Bernard Weinraub, "GOP, Buoyed by Response to Ads, Plans to Expand TV Campaign," *New York Times*, June 15, 1980.

[11] Gillis Long, Preface, *Rebuilding the Road to Opportunity: A Democratic Direction for the 1980s*, Mike Synar Papers, Carl Albert Center, Box 6, Folder 26. See Brandt (2007) for a discussion of how the Committee on Party Effectiveness and the issue-agenda initiative emerged from New Democrat activity after 1980.

The Democrats' final product in 1982 was a 135-page book titled *Rebuilding the Road to Opportunity: A Democratic Direction for the 1980s*. Released in September 1982 in a cheerful bright yellow cover (some Democrats referred to it as "The Yellow Brick Road"),[12] the manifesto offered critiques of Reagan Administration policies, but it emphasized detailed review of issue priorities and specific proposals for policy directions. Central issue items included long-term economic policy, housing, small business, women's economic issues, the environment, crime, and national security. Each area was the focus of a chapter containing a report from one of the caucus task forces.[13] *Rebuilding the Road to Opportunity* presented the Democratic agenda as one that was unifying if not unanimous: "[These] are not iron clad positions which every Democrat must follow in lockstep. Rather, they represent the ideas of a broad-based group of House Democrats, reflective of all the political philosophies within our caucus."[14]

The wide-ranging agenda attracted some press attention in September. Democrats released the economics report four days before the full *Road to Opportunity*, and they enjoyed focused coverage of the economic agenda and then of other priorities. Coverage in the *New York Times* and *Washington Post* highlighted the centrist tone of the agenda's proposals – the *Times* noted that the party had "shunned the traditional Democratic liberal prescriptions such as jobs programs and credit controls to advocate more conservative approaches" – and highlighted some major new initiatives.[15] Long-term attention to the Democrats' agenda was limited, though. House Speaker Tip O'Neill would later complain that the agenda got "very little encouragement or attention from the press,"[16] and House Democrats tried to return to the *Road to Opportunity* again in the lead up to the 1984 election by forming a "National House Democratic Caucus" with congressional Democrats and outside figures to publicize the manifesto's priorities.[17]

Among the post-1980 election agendas, the Democrats' 1982 document is a particularly comprehensive attempt, both in its participatory development and

---

[12] Margot Hornblower, "House Democrats Are Feeling Feisty as 1984 Approaches," *Washington Post*, March 5, 1983.

[13] Caucus Committee on Party Effectiveness, *Rebuilding the Road to Opportunity: A Democratic Direction for the 1980s*, Mike Synar Papers, Carl Albert Center, Box 6, Folder 26.

[14] Long, Preface, *Rebuilding the Road to Opportunity: A Democratic Direction for the 1980s*.

[15] "Democrats Unveil a 'New' Look," *New York Times*, September 22, 1982; Margot Hornblower, "House Democrats Tackle the Issues Again – Generally," *Washington Post*, September 23, 1982.

[16] Bill Peterson, "House Democrats Launch Effort to Sell Alternatives to the Public," *Washington Post*, July 20, 1983.

[17] "Top Democrats Form National Caucus to Promote Unified Party Program," press release, July 19, 1983, Synar Collection, Box 20, Folder 47; James F. Clarity and William E. Farrell, "Democrats on the Road," *New York Times*, November 28, 1983.

in its detailed discussion of priorities and solutions. In its content, it demonstrates a leadership response to the losses of 1980, with a strategic tack toward the center. In its presentation, the book length format was the polar opposite of the Republicans' pithy 1980 announcement and the concise checklist of the 1994 Contract with America. In that sense, the 1982 agenda was an evolutionary dead end, but as a concrete, electorally targeted congressional agenda, it was a harbinger of things to come.

1996 Democrats

Because of the power of presidential party leadership (Galvin 2010), congressional issue agendas issued by parties that control the White House appear to have received limited attention. The Democrats' "Families First" agenda is such a case, issued during the 1996 election cycle as Bill Clinton sought reelection. The 1996 example, like the 1982 agenda, shows a congressional party crafting a strategic pitch to key voters, but in contrast to 1982, the 1996 Democrats could draw lessons in framing from the 1994 Republican Contract. As a presidential-year congressional agenda, the Families First agenda stands out for the relatively close coordination between the House minority party and the White House: some items in the congressional agenda were already Clinton proposals, and the Families First agenda even lent its name to the 1996 Democratic National Convention and some of its content to the national party platform.[18]

Democratic leaders coordinated agenda development within the caucus, evaluating about 120 suggested policy proposals and consulting with groups, including the conservative Blue Dogs.[19] The final product stressed themes of responsibility, security, and opportunity, and proposed twenty-one specific policy items that reflected electoral targeting "with an eye toward winning support of conservative Democrats and moderate Republicans."[20] These included the promise of a balanced budget, tax cuts for small businesses, and childcare tax credits.

The agenda's public rollout was a team effort between House Minority Leader Dick Gephardt (D-MO) and Senate Minority Leader Tom Daschle (D-SD). The party leaders staged a satellite linkup with Democratic incumbents and challengers in Des Moines, Detroit, Houston, and Sacramento to promote

---

[18] "Families First," *Washington Post*, June 24, 1996; Ruth Marcus, "Democrats Avoiding Dissent Over Platform," *Washington Post*, July 11, 1996; Richard Berke, "Democrats Lay Claim to Family Values," *New York Times*, August 28, 1996.

[19] Dan Balz, "Gephardt: Party Has Learned Its Lessons," *Washington Post*, September 16, 1996; Jennifer Bradley, "For Blue Dog Dems, There's Strength in Small Numbers," *Roll Call*, August 29, 1996.

[20] Quote from Christopher Georges, "Democrats' 'Families First' Agenda Gets Tepid Support from Candidates," *Wall Street Journal*, June 24, 1996.

the agenda and earn media attention.[21] Gephardt consistently framed the agenda as practical and centrist: he described it variously as "modest, moderate, and feasible" and "moderate, sensible, and realistic."[22] This appeal to voters dissatisfied with the unpopular Republican Congress generally received "strong backing across the party's ideological lines,"[23] although the leadership did not seek or receive the lockstep unity that Republicans achieved with the 1994 Contract. During the fall campaign, some House liberals undermined pledges like the balanced budget item, and some Democratic candidates distanced themselves from the agenda effort, citing their own independence from party leaders.[24]

In the 1996 Democratic agenda, we see a congressional party again responding to loss, but doing so in the context of a presidentially centered campaign. Congressional leaders generated an agenda aimed at the most persuadable voters, and developed themes that meshed with the centrist Clinton campaign. While Democrats failed to retake the House or Senate, Clinton easily won reelection and continued to pursue the themes from the 1996 campaign. Interestingly, the congressional leadership and the White House worked together in 2000 on an agenda with similar issue concerns and a familiar name: Families First 2000.[25]

2010 Republicans

Congressional Republicans headed into the 2010 elections with the usual midterm advantages, enhanced by the energy of Tea Party activism and partisan outrage at the passage of the Affordable Care Act. Seeking to retake the majority they had lost in 2006, Republicans formed a plan to develop an election agenda. The initial planning, led by Kevin McCarthy (R-CA) starting in May, included an "America Speaking Out" project that solicited public input through town hall meetings and a website through which voters could propose agenda items and vote other proposals up or down.[26]

---

[21] John Yang, "Hill Democrats Borrow a Few Themes for Center-Looking 'Families First' Agenda," *Washington Post*, June 23, 1996.

[22] Yang, "Hill Democrats Borrow"; Benjamin Sheffner, "Democrats Will Unveil Own 'Contract' on June 23 at Five Regional Locations," *Roll Call*, June 13, 1996.

[23] Yang, "Hill Democrats Borrow."

[24] Ed Kilgore, "'New Democrats' Key to Steering Bipartisan Course in the 105th," *Roll Call*, October 3, 1996; Georges, "Democrats' 'Family First' Agenda."

[25] "Families First: The 2000 Democratic Agenda," clintonwhitehouse6.archives.gov/2000/02/2000-02-10-fact-sheet-on-the-2000-democratic-agenda.html.

[26] Jackie Kucinich, "GOP Web Project Contributed Little to Pledge," *Roll Call*, September 27, 2010; Archived "America Speaking Out" website, https://web.archive.org/web/20100530065624/ http://www.americaspeakingout.com/.

The leadership unveiled the final agenda in September at a fairly low-key event at a lumberyard in Virginia.[27] The full "Pledge to America" filled forty-five pages and identified key action items that centered largely on "the tenets of mainstream conservatism over the last generation," as the *New York Times* described it.[28] The proposals included cuts to spending, Affordable Care Act repeal, and caps on federal hiring, as well as new spending on missile defense. Many of these conventionally conservative positions followed directly from major legislation that key Republican House members had introduced earlier in the 111th Congress.[29] The agenda minimized cultural issues, although it did call for making the antiabortion Hyde Amendment permanent, and the far right House members were dissatisfied with the absence of issues like immigration.[30] The Pledge to America further appealed to the energized base of the party by adopting some limited-government planks, including proposals to require citation of constitutional authority for all legislation and to limit omnibus legislation.[31] The agenda, overall, seemed to mix appeals to core conservative issues with strategic but largely symbolic pitches to Tea Party Republicans.[32]

Just after rolling out the agenda, Republicans followed up on the House floor by using procedural maneuvers to force votes on some items, such as the promise to shut down the Troubled Asset Relief Program (TARP).[33] Then in November, of course, Republicans returned to majority control with a decisive win. While they did not stage the very high-profile sweep of early legislation that some other modern midterm agendas motivated, the Pledge to America themes directly connected to the main priorities of the Republican 112th Congress, and Republican leaders followed through specifically on some of their Tea Party-esque promises about the legislative process.[34]

---

[27] David Herszenhorn, "GOP Agenda to Take House Pushes Tax Cut," *New York Times*, September 23, 2010.

[28] Jackie Kucinich and Kathleen Hunter, "Battle Begins Over Republican Pledge," *Roll Call*, September 30, 2010; David Herszenhorn, "Legislative Plan Direct from GOP Mainstream," *New York Times*, September 24, 2010.

[29] Kucinich, "GOP Web Project."

[30] Steven T. Dennis, "Republicans Tussle Over What 'Pledge' Doesn't Say," *Roll Call*, September 30, 2010.

[31] Paul Kane and Perry Bacon, Jr., "GOP's Agenda Aims to Shrink Government," *Washington Post*, September 23, 2010; Kucinich, "GOP Web Project."

[32] The advantage of appealing to Tea Party concerns was likely obvious to leaders already, but Tea Party activists made their agenda clear by creating a 10-item "Contract from America" based on an online ballot system in early 2010. Bernie Becker, "A Revised Contract for America, Minus 'With' and Newt," *New York Times*, April 14, 2010.

[33] Kucinich and Hunter, "Battle Begins Over Republican Pledge."

[34] David Fahrenthold, "In House, GOP Invokes Constitution," *Washington Post*, September 17, 2011.

2.1.3 Summary

In the polarizing, highly competitive period since 1980, congressional party election agendas have become commonplace. The parties have varied in the intensity of these messaging efforts, as well as in the way that they developed strategically aimed issue proposals for electoral purposes. The balance of leadership and rank-and-file involvement has varied, too. Some cases involved long-term engagement by many members in formulating an agenda, as in the 1982 example, while others seem to have been driven more by strategic leadership choices with member involvement for buy-in, as in 2010. Political context has mattered a great deal for whether agendas are offered – the 1982 agenda being a rare majority case – and parties in the White House (1996) and in presidential election years (1980, 1996) have needed to coordinate with the presidential ticket to achieve any attention.

Overall, the post-1980 parties have devoted the most energy to election agendas in midterm cycles when they were entirely out of power – and these are the cases in which the potential relationship between agendas and later policy priorities are strongest. In the sections that follow, I turn to the 1994 Republican and 2006 Democratic agendas as more detailed case studies of agenda development and postelection agenda action. As examples that emerged from the most favorable political circumstances for party unity, widespread attention, and strategic success, these two cases allow me to explore the nature of agenda formation and consequences in the context where we should see the greatest incentives for agenda promotion and follow-through.

2.2 Competition, Messaging, and Legislating

Congressional scholarship has no shortage of attention to agendas, broadly defined. We know the importance of agenda control to the power of the majority party (Cox and McCubbins 2005), how that power came to be centered in the Speaker and other majority leadership (Stewart and Jenkins 2013), and how it may vary contextually (Rohde 1991; Sinclair 1995; Smith 2007). Agenda research has established the strategic use of floor agendas to build the majority party's external political support (Gelman 2020; Harbridge 2015). Other important work documents how the congressional agenda absorbs important policy problems and how institutional factors shape that process (e.g., Adler and Wilkerson 2012). The connection between national party campaigns and legislative agendas has drawn less attention. In this section, I situate the rise of national congressional campaign agendas in the changing politics of the current era, and I consider lessons from research on party platforms and manifestos for how to understand the formation and effects of these agendas.

Sharply rising polarization and the new normal of constant competition for congressional majority control has brought about new incentives for the parties. As Frances Lee has demonstrated, party "teamsmanship" is now a driving force in Congress, and the electoral fate of the party team has risen to the top of the party's priorities in the last quarter century or so (Lee 2009). With control of the Senate seemingly up for grabs since 1980, and control of the House in question virtually every two years since 1994, the threshold goal of gaining or keeping majority control now motivates much of what the congressional party does (Heberlig and Larson 2012; Lee 2016).

Message-centered politics is a primary result as the party seeks to use the lawmaking process and legislative institutions to convey its electoral issue priorities. Minority parties use procedural prerogatives and public actions to articulate alternatives to the majority (Green 2015). The parties compete to communicate messages through floor speeches on major issues (Hughes and Koger 2022) and in their use of amendments (Theriault 2015). Parties have retooled their staffing and organizations to emphasize public messaging, even at the expense of policymaking resources (Lee 2016; Meinke 2016). And the partisan imperative has directly shaped the congressional floor agenda, as party leaders craft the floor agenda to send signals to external audiences (Harbridge 2015).

As congressional polarization and electoral competition have risen, American politics has also *nationalized* to a significant extent (Hopkins 2018). The candidate-centered congressional elections of the mid- to late-twentieth century have eroded, and with them much of the incumbent advantage. Jacobson argues that incumbency has weakened with more nationalized politics and the "rise in party loyalty and straight-ticket voting" that has followed from the "widening and increasingly coherent partisan divisions in the American electorate" (Jacobson 2015, 861–862). In turn, the nationalized political climate strengthens the link between the party brand and the trajectory of the congressional party (Jones 2015), and the congressional agenda may shape the agenda and brand of the national party (Fagan 2021).

It would be easy to conclude that highly competitive, nationalized politics centered on messaging has become decoupled from lawmaking and policy outcomes – that parties primarily seeking electorally useful imagery do so without serious legislating. As Lee (2017, 139) notes, "enacting legislation is simply not essential to partisan public relations," and "there are many circumstances when legislative failure is more advantageous to a party's majority-seeking aims." Yet partisan messaging can connect with lawmaking over the long term in ways that have important implications for representation. Gelman shows that the majority party strategically trades off floor agenda space between lawmaking and "dead on arrival" (DOA) messaging bills (Gelman 2020). These DOA messaging bills represent commitments to party-supporting groups, and some DOA bills are eventually enacted after the party seizes unified government control. In this sense, messaging in the legislative process is in part a long-range promise to parts of the party coalition.

Congressional election agendas are, in the same way, a party action that distinctly blends majority-seeking party messaging with concrete promises of future legislative action. They are places where we can see both the changing incentives of nationalizing politics motivating messaging and the emerging representational implications of those messages in practice. The agendas have the potential to shape congressional representation as they modify, at least under some circumstances, the nature of promissory representation (Mansbridge 2003) in Congress. Tracy Sulkin's research establishes that members are individually responsive in their Washington activity to the issue agenda priorities of their own campaigns and those of their challengers (Sulkin 2005, 2011; see also Russell and Wen 2021). As congressional campaigns become less coupled to local concerns, we may expect members and their party leaders to respond to national agenda content in representation as well, particularly since there is evidence that party messaging can successfully frame parties' images with voters (Somer-Topcu, Tavits, and Baumann 2020). Moreover, voters distinguish between broad position-taking messages and concrete *promises* from candidates, as Bonilla (2022) shows, finding the latter to be far more motivating.[35] The congressional parties' national promises may have a similar effect to the candidate promises in Bonilla's work, and they may in turn motivate the kind of party-level response that Sulkin finds from individual incumbents.

2.3 Lessons from Platforms and Manifestos

Research on party platforms and manifestos provides further context for the emerging role of congressional party agendas. Like platforms, modern congressional election agendas signal priorities and contain policy promises, and the party uses the policy content strategically as an electoral appeal.[36] While the congressional agendas are much more limited and selective than national or state platforms in the United States or manifestos in other countries, the research on these documents points toward parties' strategic choices in formulating agendas and the ways in which they map onto later policymaking.

---

[35] Royed, Baldwin, and Borrelli (2019) in turn find evidence that specific pledges from US presidential election platforms are fulfilled at a fairly high rate.

[36] Here, both platforms and congressional election agendas might be contrasted with image-based party electoral appeals that are either devoid of overt issue content or even contradict platform positions (Philpot 2007).

We can learn from this work that there is considerable variability in *how platforms are produced*, with some parties exhibiting more inclusivity in developing agendas than others (Harmel 2018; also see Caillaud and Tirole 1999). In the United States, some national party platforms have emerged from a fairly closed process (Harmel 2018, 233), but recent evidence depicts a more permeable process that is unevenly influenced by some groups. Within the extended party network of Democratic policy demanders, Victor and Reinhardt (2018) find that more loyal groups and groups located near the party's ideological center have more influence on the Democratic national platform. In the comparative context, variation in the diversity of the party itself is associated with more diverse platform content, as Greene and O'Brien (2016) show with gender diversity in the legislative party (see also Kittilson 2010). The content of platforms is also shaped by strategic considerations. In particular, parties are not only deciding on issue positions, which reflect party "identity," but also deciding on the party "image" portrayed to the mass electorate, embodied in the relative emphasis on different issues (Harmel et al. 2018). We know that in the US context, the positions and their emphasis are contested in party messages. In his research on the party committees' public efforts, Heersink shows that the parties – especially when out of power – work to define national brands, sometimes experiencing significant conflict over the content of those brand messages (Heersink 2018).

Students of platforms have also explored the *impact of platforms on legislative action and policy outputs*. Platforms inevitably compete with other agenda-shapers, particularly short-term public issue priorities and media attention. But comparative work suggests that manifestos predict at least a portion of legislative activity for majority parties or coalitions (Borghetto and Belchior 2020; Brouard et al. 2018; Froio, Bevan, and Jennings 2017). Work that takes a broad view of policy implementation in the United Kingdom finds a relationship between winning party manifestos and policy promise-keeping (Bara 2005). In the United States, Fagan builds directly on comparative manifesto research to examine how national Democratic and GOP platforms predict congressional activity in subsequent Congresses (Fagan 2018). Coding the content of platforms, he finds that the president's party platform predicts congressional roll call and committee attention, conditional on unified government.

Party platforms may also influence perceptions of mandates and, in turn, representational decisions in Congress. The concept of electoral mandates is a complicated one (Azari 2014), and while it is difficult to attribute decisive mandates to American elections, legislators may perceive mandates in ways that affect their behavior. Evidence from the 1994 Contract with America and from the 1980 election shows that many members bend their voting behavior, for limited periods of time, in the direction of a perceived mandate (Peterson et al. 2003). This connection helps demonstrate how congressional agendas can affect legislative politics despite low public awareness. Just before the 1994 election, about seven of ten voters had not even heard of the Contract with America, so little of the dramatic election outcome can be attributed to it directly (Jacobson 1996). Yet the Contract remained quite important to how the leadership and members talked about and perceived the results of the election.

2.4 Cases and Expectations

In what follows in Sections 3 and 4, I turn to the 1994 Contract with America and the 2006 New Direction for America to examine the party's agenda choices and their relationship to subsequent legislating. Here, I outline expectations for the empirical study of those two cases. A word about the choice of the Contract and New Direction for study is in order first. As the background in the first part of this section illustrates, these two campaigns both represent the out-of-power, midterm election cases that have tended to motivate major agenda efforts. These are not, then, chosen as a representative sample of agenda attempts since 1980, and the findings may not generalize to other cases with different contexts and configurations of power. Instead, these two cases allow a view of what agenda-centered campaigning – and subsequent governing – looks like when a congressional party's leadership perceives strong strategic value in a national agenda and commits to that agenda in the campaign. In considering the legislative consequences of these agendas after the campaign, we can see what the relationship between the national campaign and House governing looks like at its maximum potential.

The sections on the Contract and New Direction agendas begin with a review of the agendas' origins. Like mini-platforms, these agendas selectively outline priorities based on strategic considerations. How do congressional parties select these priorities, and whose concerns do they strategically represent? House parties are made up of divergent groups, and a concise agenda represents a decision to prioritize some factions' issues over others. In its other agenda-setting decisions, congressional leadership is always constrained by the preferences of rank-and-file members (Rohde 1991), but leaders also find some leeway within party differences to make strategic and entrepreneurial decisions (Strahan 2007). I argue that the construction of election agendas follows a similar pattern. Taking into consideration expressed rank-and-file priorities, the accountable congressional leaders make final decisions about the electoral strategy behind the document and the final priorities in the agenda that follow from that strategy.

In making these choices, leaders select a package of issues that will appeal to their electoral target in the election. This strategic selectivity means that some segments of the party caucus – those whose interests coincide with the party's strategy – should find their issues better represented in the agenda. Which elements of the caucus "win" in the agenda will depend on the electoral context. As the two parties look out over nationalized congressional contests, they will see that context differently depending on the party and the election cycle. I examine the representation of intraparty interests defined by both *ideological positioning* and *electoral vulnerability* in the study of 1994 and 2006, although strategic agenda content could be targeted at other subsets of the caucus as well.

The platform and manifesto research discussed in Section 2.3 demonstrates that pledges in election agendas relate to policy activity after the election, in part because of legislators' perceptions that the agenda is connected to their party's electoral success. I expect that the priorities set in major congressional election agendas will influence legislating in the House in two ways. First, following the general approach that Fagan (2018) uses to study US national party platforms, I expect that overall attention to agenda-related topics will increase after the election, both in committee processes (hearings) and in floor processes (roll-call votes). The decision to shift substantially toward agenda issues is not necessarily without cost, since agenda issue attention will crowd out committee consideration and floor time for other priorities. However, the party's public commitment and members' perception of a mandate for these issues should incline the party's membership toward these priorities and give committee and floor leaders a strong claim to prioritizing the issues.

Beyond the broad shift in attention, we should expect House majorities that won after an agenda-focused campaign to take specific legislative actions to follow through on the agenda's pledges. As we would also expect, and as I will show, the impact of those actions on policy outcomes will be constrained by the bicameral and separation-of-powers contexts.

2.5 Methods

In the sections on the Contract with America and New Direction for America, I draw on multiple methods and a range of data sources to establish the process of agenda development, to compare the issues in each agenda with member and leadership priorities, and to track the issues in the agenda in the legislative process after the elections. The approach builds on qualitative and quantitative analysis to create a broad picture and evaluate the main expectations, not resting on any single test or data source for the conclusions.

2.5.1 Agenda Formation

To trace how House Republicans and Democrats arrived at these two election agendas, I present qualitative process evidence drawn from archived papers, archived websites, and contemporaneous reporting and analysis. For the 1994 Contract, have I relied on the extensive Newt Gingrich Congressional Papers, examining the files related to the Contract itself and to party leadership and planning in the years before and after the 1994 election. Internal memos, presentations, and notes on planning were particularly helpful in understanding the process and the role of rank-and-file members. Additional archival evidence came from the papers of Tom DeLay (R-TX) and Dick Armey (R-TX). I have supplemented the archival evidence with details from media reporting and with several secondary sources that described and analyzed Contract processes during or shortly after the 104th Congress.[37]

For the 2006 Democratic agenda, archival sources are currently limited in availability. Papers from retired Representative David Obey (D-WI) provided a small amount of very useful agenda information, but much of the process information was assembled from media coverage and archived party web pages. Archived web pages also provided additional information on the public presentation of the agenda.

2.5.2 Agenda Content and Priorities

To study the relationship between the priorities of members, agenda content, and legislative activity, I began by coding the policy issue content of each agenda using the Policy Agendas Project coding scheme for major and subtopic issue coding. For the Contract, detailed documents were maintained by the Republican Conference that tracked how each issue promise in the Contract mapped onto later House legislation.[38] To identify the issue priorities of the Contract, I used the issue codes for those legislative measures. The Appendix lists the Contract issue areas and the major and subtopic issue codes.

---

[37] Media searches for the 1994 and 2006 cases, as well as for the example cases discussed in Section 2, cast a broad net using the agenda name and variations on it (e.g., "New Direction," "New Direction for America," "Six for '06") as search terms during a time span including the election year as well as the first year of the subsequent Congress. Searches targeted the *New York Times*, the *Washington Post*, *Roll Call*, *Politico* (2007 and after), and *CQ Weekly*.

[38] House Republican Conference Fact Sheet, Enactment of the Bills of the Contract with America: An Update, September 23, 1997, Newt Gingrich Papers, University of West Georgia, Ingram Library Special Collections, Box 2132, Folder: Contract with America; "Contract Score Card." The term limits constitutional amendment in the Contract reached the floor as a joint resolution, which does not receive coding in the Congressional Bills Project data, and it is coded manually based on its topic focus.

A similar document was not available as the basis for the New Direction issue coding. Democrats passed a very limited set of bills (HR 1 through HR 6) as part of a "100 hours" version of the Six for '06, but the major and subtopic codes of these few broad bills represent only a narrow slice of the agenda content, particularly in subtopics. Though the party went on to take further action on agenda issues later in the Congress, the leadership did not maintain an agenda-centered tracking document like the Republican Conference did. To capture the scope of the issue promises in the New Direction, I coded each sentence of the policy statements in the six categories (two to seven sentences per category) of the agenda summary that was released in late summer of 2006,[39] classifying them according to the major and subtopic codes in the Policy Agendas Project coding (see Appendix for a full list of codes).

To determine how individual members' priorities were represented in the agendas, I examine bill introductions using Policy Agendas Project bills data (Adler and Wilkerson 2019) in the Congresses leading up to the 1994 and 2006 elections. Bill introductions have good potential for identifying member issue priorities within each party. Recent work on the 101st–111th Congresses shows considerable intraparty variation in sponsorship priorities. Similarly, rising polarization has not led to a clear differentiation overall between the parties in issue priorities (Sulkin and Schmitt 2014). For this analysis, data on individual introductions were collapsed into a data set organized with the member-Congress as the unit of analysis, summing total introductions by member as well as introductions in the Contract and New Direction major topics and subtopics.

While bill introductions highlight the revealed issue priorities of *individual members*, I turn to other indicators to examine whether the agenda's issue focus was foreshadowed by the *minority-party leadership's choices* in the House before the election. Data on topics and subtopics in motions to recommit indicate the minority leadership's priorities in procedural messaging. And data on topics in members' one-minute floor speeches – individual activities that are coordinated by the party leadership – reveal leadership priorities and members' individual participation in those priorities.[40]

2.5.3 Legislative Activity and Outcomes

Understanding the party's postelection legislative attention to agenda topics requires data on issue priorities in the legislative process. To understand

---

[39] Coding based on content of six agenda areas in "A New Direction for America," September 1, 2006, HouseDemocrats.gov via archive.org, July 4, 2019. web.archive.org/web/20061129202443/ http://www.democraticleader.house.gov/pdf/thebook.pdf.

[40] Data on floor speeches was provided by Tyler Hughes (2018), and the data on floor motions is from the PIPC data set (Crespin and Rohde 2022).

broad changes in legislative priorities, I use aggregate data on all House committee hearings as well as all nonprocedural House roll-call votes to check for increased focus on agenda issues after the election. Using data on House hearings and nonprocedural roll-call votes from the Policy Agendas Project (2019), I track the numbers and relative share of hearings and votes given to agenda topics before and after the 1994 and 2006 elections. To consider specific actions on agenda promises, I also track the progress of major agenda-related legislation in the 104th and 110th Congresses, and I compare the major enactments of these two Congresses with the priorities of the election agendas. Data sources for these analyses are described with the corresponding discussion.

3 Republicans: The 1994 Contract with America

3.1 Origins

The 1994 midterm elections presented Republicans with a distinct opportunity to make major gains in their pursuit of a House majority, though few anticipated the fifty-two-seat surge that would take them to the majority in the 104th Congress (Green and Crouch 2022, 105). The GOP had picked up ten House seats in the 1992 election but remained dozens of seats away from a majority in the 103rd Congress. But President Clinton's tumultuous first two years and plummeting popularity through 1994 provided the short-term context for Republicans to build on favorable long-term trends and seize the House majority for the first time in four decades. In this context, Republicans "succeeded in framing the local choice in national terms" (Jacobson 1996), in part through the national agenda offered in the September 1994 rollout of the Contract with America. The Contract featured specific promises for legislative action in each of ten issue areas, including budget reform, crime, welfare, family policy, tax cuts, regulatory reform, defense, social security, legal reform, and term limits.[41]

In the broadest sense, the Contract with America had its roots in Newt Gingrich's goals – and his preference for corporate style, long-range strategy. Gingrich had aggressively promoted an ideological, message-oriented plan for a Republican majority with his "Conservative Opportunity Society" group (COS) in the 1980s, and he had advocated agenda-centered national campaigns at least as early as 1980.[42] Some of the issues and themes in the

---

[41] Contract with America Briefing Book, September 1994, Newt Gingrich Congressional Papers, University of West Georgia, Ingram Library Special Collections, Box 1977, unlabeled folder.

[42] As discussed in Section 2.1.2, Gingrich pushed for a Capitol-steps announcement by Ronald Reagan and congressional Republicans in 1980, which was, in the end, narrowly focused on the Kemp-Roth tax cut plan.

1994 Contract can be traced back to the issue activity of the COS in the early
Reagan era (Green and Crouch 2022, 36). Gingrich's designs on
a nationalized, conservative congressional majority, as several scholars
have demonstrated (Green and Crouch 2022; Strahan 2007; Zelizer 2020),
were developed at his initiative over a long period of time, and they represent a clear case of individual agency in congressional leadership. Gingrich
seized on broader political shifts to mobilize his conference and the larger
Republican Party, shaping how and when polarization and nationalization
changed congressional party leadership. Thus the origins of the Contract
should be understood both in context and as a part of distinctly Gingrichian
agency.[43]

Gingrich's election as minority whip in a closely contested 1989 race
placed him in a position to influence party planning more directly, and he
quickly retooled parts of the Republican whip organization to pursue long-
term goals. With his "strategy whip" group, Gingrich was considering
a "campaign pact" and even an announcement on the Capitol steps for the
1992 election cycle.[44] At that time, though, Gingrich's attempts ran up against
other power centers in the caucus.[45] Meanwhile, Gingrich was actively
building a base of support from the ground up. His GOPAC funding operation
in the late 1980s and early 1990s emphasized candidate recruitment and
"relentlessly inculcating" candidates with COS messaging via widely distributed audiotapes (Rae 1998, 22–23).[46] GOPAC recruited more conservative
candidates in safe districts, and GOPAC targets in 1992 proved to be more
loyal to Gingrich after the election (Asmussen Mathew and Kunz 2017).

With the participation of the energetic class of freshman Republicans he had
helped to recruit, Gingrich stepped up his messaging focus in the 103rd
Congress (1993–94) (Koopman 1996, 141). For the 1994 midterms, Gingrich
began early in the cycle with a renewed effort to assemble a concise and widely
publicized agenda. In winter 1994, the Republican Conference met at Salisbury
University for a strategic retreat. Members heard from party leaders and experts
and had an opportunity to voice their particular priorities for the election themes

---

[43] See Strahan (2007) on Gingrich as a consequential actor, and see Childs and Krook (2009) on the
related argument for critical actors in motivating policy change.
[44] Strategy Whip Meeting Agenda, July 8, 1992, Gingrich Papers, Box 2684, Folder: Wednesday
Morning Meeting. President Bush also rebuffed an attempt to reprise the 1980 coordinated
campaign event in 1992 (Green and Crouch 2022, 91).
[45] Steve Gunderson to Gingrich, June 6, 1991, Gingrich Papers, Box 2663, Folder: January 1991.
[46] Gingrich's work within the Republican Conference to coordinate electoral themes and sharpen
partisan divisions in campaigns extended across almost his entire House career. As a NRCC
member in the mid-80s, and then as the leader of GOPAC, Gingrich pushed consistently for more
nationalized campaigns and provided messaging resources for candidates (Green and Crouch
2022, 44, 57, 67, 85).

in full sessions and in small groups.[47] Republican pollster Frank Luntz advised the caucus to run an agenda-centered campaign and not to rely solely on opposition to President Clinton, and he specifically identified a set of issues at the top of public concern, including crime, welfare reform, and education, among others.[48]

According to John Boehner (R-OH), then a second-term member, "The retreat was pretty rocky at first. . . Some people thought that we were questioning their Republicanism. But we focused on what we had in common, our goals and how to get there."[49] The "rocky" discussion featured free-flowing input from many members who emphasized a wide range of priorities, including some that became central to the Contract (crime, education) and others that notably did not (health care, trade, immigration).[50]

Along with the open discussion of issue priorities, the conference discussion led to support for a general plan for a "ten-point positive agenda" for the election, and ratification of five broad conservative themes that would guide the later stages of the process (Strahan 2007, 145). These "guiding principles" that emerged from conference discussion were "individual liberty, limited government, economic opportunity, personal responsibility, and security at home and abroad" (Bader 1996, 180).

Following the early 1994 conference, House Republican leaders gradually developed a plan for assembling an agenda with a Capitol-steps rollout in September. The Contract would unfold in a "two-stage process" involving, first, decisions over "which items to include," and then over "how to sell it to the public" (Rae 1998, 23). Gingrich delegated agenda-content planning to Dick Armey (R-TX), who in turn created a permeable process that drew a range of "activist" members of the conference, according to contemporaneous interviews by Daniel Stid (Stid 1996; see also Strahan 2007, 145).

Groups of members and staff worked on refining general messages and themes after the Salisbury conference for testing.[51] The Contract's general framework was adopted early on – a set of day-one items plus ten priorities for the first 100 days. The specific priorities were informed primarily by surveys

[47] Salisbury Conference Draft Agenda, January 11, 1994, Gingrich Papers, Box 2629, Folder: Planning and Strategy Memos (1). Also see Stid (1996).

[48] Frank Luntz, From Minority to Majority: A Strategy for the Republican House Leadership, January 27, 1994, Gingrich Papers, Box 2629, Folder: Planning and Strategy Memos (2).

[49] Quotation from Daniel Stid (1996, 6), who observed Contract implementation from Dick Armey's office in the 104th Congress, and conducted interviews with key players in its development.

[50] Congress of Tomorrow Members Report, January 27, 1994, Gingrich Papers, Box 2629, Folder: Planning and Strategy Memos (1).

[51] Jerry Climer to John Boehner, Jim Nussle, Pete Hoekstra and various staff, April 19, 1994, Gingrich Papers, Box 2629, Folder: Planning and Strategy Memos (1).

of both incumbent Republicans and GOP challengers as well as by meetings with "allies" (the extended party) and party officials.[52] The internal survey work asked members and candidates to evaluate "the desirability and political feasibility of more than 60 potential legislative initiatives" as well as to rank a set of general issue priorities (Bader 1996, 186). Inside the Republican Conference, incumbents had opportunities for formal input at Contract-focused forums and meetings of the House Republican Policy Committee, although these forums were not always well attended – because many GOP members "simply didn't take the project seriously" in mid-1994, according to Armey staffer Kerry Knott (Gimpel 1996, 19). Meanwhile, party-aligned external groups, such as the Heritage Foundation and the Christian Coalition, contributed policy details (Koopman 1996, 145). A key Gingrich priority was ensuring that the proposals "excited the outside groups associated with the party" (Stid 1996, 6).

With the Contract's agenda items lining up, the Armey-led process turned to legislative details in the summer. The working groups, including key Republican committee members, framed model legislation for each Contract priority (Gimpel 1996, 18–19; Green and Crouch 2022, 104). Choosing this level of policy detail meant that House Republicans had to sort though sometimes deep differences on issue specifics. One of the most challenging areas was the Contract proposal for welfare reform. The welfare reform working group was split over a major reform bill sponsored by Rick Santorum (R-PA), which already had broad support in the House GOP. Gingrich and Armey preferred a more hard-line bill that severely limited federal spending and permitted denial of state benefits to unwed parents (Gimpel 1996, 82–83; Strahan 2007, 157–158). The Gingrich/Armey approach won out – and, as Strahan argues, the conservative resolution of conflicts over Contract content demonstrates the latitude that Gingrich found to maneuver a divided party in the direction of his own vision (Strahan 2007, 152–165).

Given the Contract's reputation as a poll-tested instrument, it is notable that candidate and member input was the focus through summer 1994, although Frank Luntz's polls and focus groups heavily shaped the final presentation. This was the second element of the two-stage process. Most phrases in the Contract "earned significant majorities" in a national survey, and the ordering of items was based on the preferences of a focus group of independents and Perot voters.[53] The titles of the Contract elements and their associated legislation reflected polled and focus-grouped wording (Rae 1998, 23). The Contract's term-limits proposal, according to Gimpel, became "The Citizen Legislature

---

[52] The Coming GOP Majority slides, undated, Gingrich Papers, Box 1977, unlabeled folder.

[53] Contract with America Briefing Book, September 1994, Gingrich Papers, Box 1977, unlabeled folder.

Act" after poll respondents favored a positive "citizen legislature" argument for term limits over a more negative argument about out-of-touch "professional politicians" (Gimpel 1996, 6).

As the range of input at the initial Salisbury conference suggested, not all members agreed with the Contract's direction. Representative John Linder (R-GA) criticized the emerging Contract's content in early August, noting that "everyone getting their issue in the mix" had yielded an agenda that was too detailed, "murky and boring," and prone to Democratic attacks over the details.[54] Retiring Republican Fred Grandy (IA) told the Washington Post, "If I were a Democrat in a closely contested district, I'd be in church right now giving thanks," because the Contract was made of proposals that "overpromise" and "underdeliver."[55]

The end result, revealed on September 27 at the Capitol event and published prominently in the *TV Guide*, was a set of congressional reforms[56] and ten legislative priorities focused on taxes, crime, education, welfare reform, and other Republican positions that could appeal both to conservatives and to Luntz-targeted disaffected voters.[57] Notably, the Contract avoided directly addressing social issues (Kabaservice 2012, 376), reflecting Gingrich's preference for positions that "did not divide the Republican conference" (Stid 1996, 6). The Contract featured a less divisive promise of a $500-per-child tax credit, though, in order "to appease Christian conservatives" (Rae 1998, 23). The Contract document also nodded to a post-Contract "expanded Republican agenda" that included, among other things, school prayer,[58] an issue had split Gingrich and Armey in the Contract's development and was left out of the Contract agenda.[59]

Once the Contract with America was out in the campaign ecosystem, Republican House candidates made individualized choices about their embrace of the agenda as part of their individual campaigns. Accounts of the 1994 campaign emphasize that many members saw the Contract as a "PR stunt" (Strahan 2007, 145) without much relevance: Joe Scarborough (R-FL) "didn't

---

[54] Linder to Gingrich and Dick Armey, August 2, 1994, Gingrich Papers, Box 1976, Folder: 2nd 100 days–Ideas. See other discussion of conflict in Koopman (1996, 146), including the view that "it was a strategic mistake to inject issues into the 1994 campaign given that Clinton's popularity and the public esteem of Congress were low."

[55] Eric Pianin, "Some in GOP Don't Buy the 'Contract,'" *Washington Post*, September 30, 1994.

[56] The day-one package of internal House reforms emerged from a much longer history of minority Republican advocacy for reform in the chamber (Harris 2019).

[57] Senate Republicans, led by an unimpressed Bob Dole (R-KS), did not provide coordinated support for the House GOP's Contract (Green and Crouch 2022, 104).

[58] Contract with America Briefing Book, September 1994, Gingrich Papers, Box 1977, unlabeled folder.

[59] Dan Balz, "GOP 'Contract' Pledges 10 Tough Acts to Follow," *Washington Post*, November 20, 1994.

mention it once" after signing it "on the very last day because the campaign committee kept faxing it to us" (Rae 1998, 24). Other candidates, though, found the Contract useful, either in its entirety or as a way to amplify some of the issue priorities they were already inclined toward in their campaign messages (Gimpel 1996, 22–28). A systematic analysis of advertising, speeches, and debates in several key 1994 races found that successful challengers varied in their use of Contract content (and GOPAC themes) (Procopio 1999). While some candidates, like Frederick Heineman (R-NC), centered their campaigns on Contract claims and Gingrich-style language, others like Brian Bilbray (R-CA) used the Contract sparingly and stressed local issues and personal factors. Comparing the Democratic incumbent campaigns, some members facing Contract-centered campaigns were thrown off their footing and found "presenting a coherent campaign message difficult," but the Contract itself could be a liability – it became fodder for advertising attacks for some incumbents (Procopio 1999, 122, 207; also see Green and Crouch 2022, 104).

Overall, the Contract's issue priorities emerged from a participatory process that tried to identify themes and issues with considerable support – but not universal consensus, particularly on the policy specifics. The process was strongly shaped by the new leadership, the conference's rising activist members, and by conservative outside groups.[60] The heavy involvement of professional pollsters, as well as the choices to exclude conservative social issues, reflect strategic decisions about an appeal to the 1994 electorate. And in the largest sense, the enterprise reflected the culmination of Gingrich's lengthy quest to define House Republicans – and, in turn, American politics – around an ideological framework.

3.2 Whose Issue Priorities?

As described in Section 2, policy agenda data can shed light on the nature of the issue priorities in congressional election agendas. Bill sponsorship activity indicates the priorities of individual members before the election and provides the basis for testing how the party strategically selected issues for the agenda. In turn, the minority leadership's message priorities in its own preelection actions should appear in its coordination of floor speeches and its decisions over floor motions. I examine each of these indicators in the following sections.

---

[60] The overall conservative direction of the Contract is illustrated well by disaffected moderate Amo Houghton (R-NY): "I'm a northeastern Republican. This thing was driven by Texas and the South. The party that I am associated with is in the tradition of Dewey, Rockefeller, Eisenhower. I am from a long family tradition of party moderates ... Northeasterners have not been invited into the inner sanctum" (quoted in Gimpel 1996, 19–20). By DW-Nominate estimates, Houghton was more liberal than 94 percent of House Republicans in 1994.

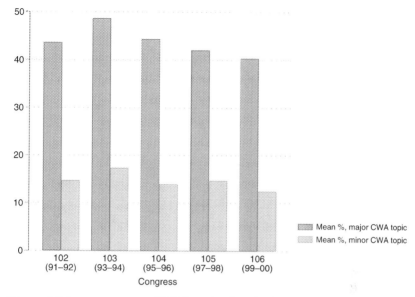

Figure 1 Mean percentage of bill introductions by GOP members on Contract policy topics

3.2.1 Member Priorities: Evidence from Bill Introductions

To study how the Contract reflected individual member priorities in the GOP conference, I have created a data set that links Contract content to House bill introductions in the 102nd–106th Congresses. To do so, I relied on the major topic and subtopic Policy Agendas Project (PAP) codes for the main legislative vehicles used to move the Contract through the House in 1995, as described in Section 2 (Adler and Wilkerson 2019). I created variables for each House Republican indicating the total bills introduced by Congress in these major and subtopic policy areas. A summary look at bill introductions shows a relative increase in Contract-related individual bill introductions in the 103rd Congress. Figure 1 shows the mean percentage of GOP bill introductions by member that corresponded to Contract policy topics, using both major and subtopic topic codings. Attention to Contract issues in individual bill sponsorship peaked with the 103rd Congress, prior to the Republican takeover. This pattern holds both for broadly defined major topics and for the specific coding of subtopics. Republican members' attention to the Contract after the 1994 election returned roughly to the levels from two Congresses before. Similarly, Figure 2 shows that Contract-related bills made up a relatively large proportion of total GOP bill introductions in the 103rd Congress, but that proportion decreased somewhat after Republicans took control in the 104th. At the big-picture level, some GOP members were emphasizing issues that then became part of the Contract prior to

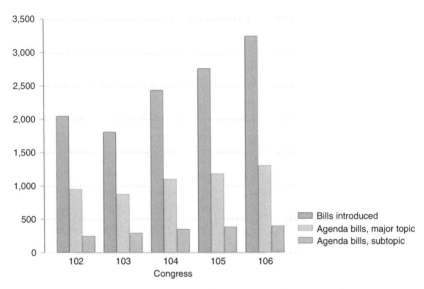

Figure 2 Total bill introductions by Republican members

the 1994 midterms, and the victory in that election did not on average spur additional sponsorship attention from individual Republicans.

Who were the Republicans who, in 1993 and 1994, had individually given more attention to issues that emerged in the fall 1994 Contract? The answer to this question can provide insight into what strategic electoral priorities the Contract served. To test explanations for members' Contract-related attention, I have modeled House Republicans' bill introduction by Congress in the 103rd Congress, using total Contract-issue introductions as the dependent variable. Negative binomial regressions are used for these models of overdispersed count data.[61] Table 2 shows the results subtopic-coded Contract bill introductions, with each member's total introductions of important bills controlled.[62] As discussed in Section 2.4, I test whether agenda items reflect issues prioritized by ideological factions (here, more conservative Republicans, as indicated by higher first-dimension DW-Nominate scores) or by more electorally vulnerable incumbents (indicated by lower GOP two-party vote share). The model also controls for members' seniority and their status as party leaders. Notably, more conservative Republicans in the 103rd Congress sponsored significantly more Contract-subtopic bills, other things held constant, and there is not a significant effect for electoral vulnerability.

---

[61] The OLS models of this data (see Online Appendix) yield substantively similar results.

[62] Analysis of the more general major-topic introductions (not shown) does not support any ideological or electoral security effects.

Table 2 House GOP bill introductions on Contract topics (subtopic PAP coding), 103rd Congress

Total impt. bills	0.069***
	(0.008)
DW-Nom. (1st)	1.858***
	(0.485)
Tenure	−0.019
	(0.021)
Top leader	0.170
	(0.315)
GOP Vote share	0.007
	(0.005)
Constant	−1.439***
	(0.430)
N	178

Negative binomial regression; Standard errors in parentheses
***$p < 0.01$

We know that the Contract reflected substantial member participation but that the party leadership structured both the process and the final decisions. Taking bill introductions as an indication of priorities and strategy, the analysis shows that it is the more conservative faction of the caucus that was emphasizing subtopics in the two years leading up to the 1994 election that would ultimately become Contract promises. This finding is consistent with what we know about changing political coalitions in this time period. For post-1980 Republicans, a pitch to new voters and districts on the basis of ideologically conservative positions should be strategically appealing. The emerging geographical base of GOP support in the south and inland west has made "the prospect of gaining seats by moving ideologically rightward ... not as counterintuitive as it might first appear" (Hopkins 2017, 158; see also Abramowitz 2018). More fundamentally, the modern Republican Party has become a distinctively ideological party (Grossmann and Hopkins 2016), playing on its advantages in symbolic conservative identification within the electorate (Ellis and Stimson 2012). In short, the agenda content is consistent with a strategy of emphasizing right-leaning priorities to appeal to conservative constituencies at a time of ongoing realignment of the parties in Congress.

3.2.2 Party-Coordinated Priorities: Evidence from Floor Speeches

House floor speeches serve as an indicator of the party leadership's coordination of messaging, and of individual members' participation in those efforts. For decades, the House morning proceedings have included alternating "one-minutes" from majority and minority-party members, delivered primarily for the C-SPAN cameras and their audience (Shogan and Glassman 2017). While members can use one-minutes for individual purposes, party leaders since the late 1980s have coordinated one-minutes to communicate party messages. Democrats and Republicans developed party structures, including the Democratic Message Board and the Republican Theme Team, to identify one-minute messages and arrange their delivery (Harris 2005, 2013).

In the early 1990s, the parties' heightened attention to one-minutes corresponded with a spike in the volume of these speeches (Shogan and Glassman 2017, 136), and the speeches have proven to be a rich source of evidence on party priorities (Hughes 2018; Hughes and Koger 2022). The majority and minority parties appear to "influence each other" (Hughes 2018, 204) in issue attention – a dynamic that yields particular opportunities for the minority party to shape the agenda in the majoritarian House. Still, research on party agenda setting in one-minutes reveals that many speeches fall outside the party's daily designated themes (Harris 2005), and one-minutes continue to provide members with opportunities to engage in representation, particularly for members who may be marginalized (Pearson and Dancey 2011). Unlike the individualized indicator of bill sponsorship, then, one-minute speeches reflect party leadership influence over messaging, but we can also view member response to that coordination since speeches remain an individual activity.

To test the relationship between Contract issues and speeches, I examine PAP major-topic coded data on floor speeches in the 103rd Congress (1993–94) (Hughes 2018).[63] In the aggregate, the minority-party Republicans foreshadowed their emphasis on Contract topics during the Congress when the agenda was developed – both parties gave substantial attention to major topics that were included in the Contract, but relative attention was much higher among Republicans, as Figure 3 illustrates. This descriptive pattern of divergence is particularly noteworthy given the tendency for the two parties to "mirror one another" in one-minute issue emphasis (Hughes and Koger 2022).

These differences were significant at the individual level: The average Republican gave 10.9 Contract-topic speeches in the 103rd Congress, compared with 5.4 for the average Democrat ($p < 0.001$). And statistically significant differences sometimes emerged *among* Republicans in Contract issue focus. The GOP members with DW-Nominate scores above the party median gave an

---

[63] See Hughes (2018) for details on the automated text classification coding used to generate this data. The one-minute data is coded only for PAP major topics.

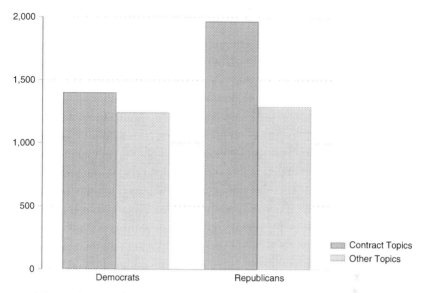

Figure 3 One-minute speeches by party, 103rd Congress (1993–94)

average of 15.5 Contract-related one-minutes, while those below the median spoke on these topics only 6.2 times ($p < 0.001$). Rough evidence of the party's coordinating role can be seen in the Gingrich-influenced "Theme Team" – its twenty-eight members delivered an average of 34.7 Contract-topic one-minutes, while other Republicans averaged 6.5 ($p < 0.001$). About 66 percent of Theme Team members' speeches addressed Contract topics, compared to 52 percent of other Republicans' speeches ($p < 0.10$).

In Table 3, I present more systematic analysis of Republican speeches in the 103rd Congress. Speech activity is very unevenly distributed among members, with many giving few one-minutes or none at all, so the modeling approach follows the one used in Section 3.2.1 for bill introductions. The negative binomial regression model includes a control for the member's total number of one-minutes in the Congress, along with the same set of predictors. Although Republicans above the party median in conservatism gave many more major Contract-topic speeches, members' Nominate scores are not predictive of speech attention in this model. Instead, we see that more junior Republicans were significantly more likely to speak on Contract topics, as were the party's top leaders.[64]

---

[64] When this data is modeled with OLS, the ideological effect rises to conventional levels of significance, and the effect for top leaders is no longer significant. Because the speeches data is overdispersed count data, I present the negative binomial results here; OLS results are available in the Online Appendix.

Table 3 House GOP one-minute speeches on Contract
topics (major-topic PAP coding), 103rd Congress

Total speeches	0.042***
	(0.003)
DW-Nom. (1st)	0.329
	(0.369)
Tenure	−0.076***
	(0.016)
Top leader	0.773***
	(0.233)
GOP Vote share	−0.002
	(0.004)
Constant	1.355***
	(0.288)
N	178

Negative binomial regression; Standard errors in parentheses
***$p < 0.01$

Overall, in the party-coordinated legislative activity of floor speaking, Republican members gave disproportionate attention to major Contract with American topics in the 103rd Congress. The minority party's efforts to shape the preelection House agenda, using one of the few tools available to it, demonstrated the importance of the issues in the conference in the time period that produced the Contract. Among Republicans, evidence of coordination around the emerging agenda follows from the emphasis on Contract topics among Theme Team members, and individual members from the junior segment of the conference were particularly likely to speak on these issues.

3.2.3 Leadership Message Priorities: Evidence from Minority-Party Motions

A third indicator, floor motions, captures minority leadership messaging on electorally advantageous issues in the legislative process. The motion to recommit in the House is distinctly important for the minority party and has long been viewed as a rare minority-empowering right in the chamber (Clark 2017). The motion is offered at the end of the floor process, after the House has ordered the previous question and before the passage vote. The motion either orders an immediate amendment to the bill (by far the most commonly used version) or simply returns the bill to committee, though Democrats eliminated the latter option in 2009.[65] House rules give the minority leader the first opportunity to offer a motion to recommit, and only one may be offered on each measure (Lynch 2011). Thus, the motion to recommit "is best thought of as a tool that is used on behalf of the minority party as a whole" (Green 2015, 171), particularly as the mechanism is available independent of Rules Committee control over content.

Minority parties have used the motion to recommit to force votes on issues that divide the majority party and/or highlight differences between the caucuses (Clark 2017). In the early 1990s, the minority's use of the motion increased sharply (Green 2015, 176). In the 103rd Congress, Republicans offered motions to recommit on 59 percent of the measures on which such a motion was in order, the highest rate of the 1990s, and a rate that would not be exceeded until the 110th Congress (2007–08) (Lynch 2011, 9).

If the motion to recommit is a tool for the minority party to signal electorally important priorities, then we might expect to see that the leadership will tailor its use of the motion to election-agenda content as that agenda is developing. In Tables 4 and 5, I compare the issue focus of motions to recommit in the 103rd Congress with other floor amendments. Data for this analysis are drawn from the Political Institutions and Public Choice (PIPC) roll-call data set (Crespin and Rohde 2022). The motions to recommit and straight amendments in the analysis include only those that received recorded roll-call votes, and the analysis excludes motions to recommit to a conference committee.

Comparing on major Contract with America topics, Republican motions to recommit significantly overrepresented Contract issues when compared with amendment votes (Table 4).[66] On Contract subtopics (Table 5), motions to recommit and floor amendments were much rarer. These topics were somewhat overrepresented on motions to recommit, although the pattern is not statistically significant.

3.2.4 Contract Priorities: Summary

Whose priorities were represented in the Republicans' 1994 Contract with America? Triangulating among the data from the 103rd Congress, we can weigh the independent issue activity of rank-and-file Republicans and the priorities of minority-party leadership in the Congress before the 1994 elections.

---

[65] For more on the types of motions to recommit and changes to the rules surrounding them, see Clark (2017) and Lynch (2011). On the role of the motion in theories of congressional party power, see Roberts (2005).

[66] By comparison, the GOP's overall floor amendment activity in the 103rd did not overrepresent Contract topics or subtopics. The GOP sponsored major-Contract-topic floor amendments at a lower rate than the Democratic majority, and there were no differences between Republicans and Democrats in sponsorship of subtopic floor amendments. Analysis of floor amendments by sponsoring party is available in the Online Appendix.

Table 4 Motions to recommit and straight amendments by Contract with America major topic, 103rd Congress

	Amendment votes	Motions to recommit	Total
Non-Contract topic	218	9	227
	50.58%	25.71%	48.71%
Contract topic	213	26	239
	49.42%	74.29%	51.29%
Total	431	35	466
	100%	100%	100%

Note: $\chi^2 = 8.01$ ($p = 0.005$)

Table 5 Motions to recommit and straight amendments by Contract with America subtopic, 103rd Congress

	Amendment votes	Motions to recommit	Total
Non-Contract subtopic	388	29	417
	90.02%	82.86%	89.48%
Contract subtopic	43	6	49
	9.98%	17.14%	10.52%
Total	431	35	466
	100%	100%	100%

Note: $\chi^2 = 1.77$ ($p = 0.184$)

At the individualized, member-controlled level, there is evidence of wide variation in attention to Contract priorities, and for subtopics, the more ideologically conservative members of the Republican Conference were more likely to introduce legislation in the 103rd Congress – evidence that the Contract's carefully crafted content was representing an appeal to conservative concerns. This analysis supports the idea that "the prospect of gaining seats by moving ideologically rightward was not as counterintuitive as it might first appear" for Republicans because of emerging geographic and ideological alignments (Hopkins 2017, 158).

At the leadership level, there is clear evidence of the party emphasizing Contract topics in actions under its control before the 1994 election. In floor speeches, which capture leadership coordination of individual behavior, Republicans heavily emphasized Contract major topics in 1993–94 relative to majority members. Comparing individual Republicans, it was the top leadership and more junior members who were more likely to speak on the agenda items under the leadership's coordination, and members of the Republican Theme

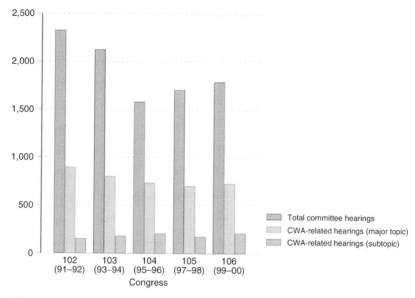

Figure 4 House committee hearings by Congress and Contract-topic coding

Team spoke very frequently on Contract topics. Finally, in leadership-controlled floor motions, we see evidence of high attention to Contract topics in 1993–94.

3.3 Consequences for Overall Legislative Activity

How much did the Contract predict the overall direction of legislative activity in the new Republican 104th Congress in committee and on the floor? To examine legislative response to the Contract and to put that response in context, I present evidence on committee hearings and floor votes. Using the same major-topic and subtopic codes, I classify House committee hearings in the 102nd–106th Congresses (Policy Agendas Project 2019). Figure 4 shows that hearings overall were down sharply in the Republican 104th Congress, but the relative share for Contract-related topics was up considerably, with close to half of the hearings falling in a major Contract-topic area. This pattern holds if full committees are analyzed alone, and it holds when both referral and nonreferral hearings are separated. In fact, the total number of referral hearings drops especially sharply from the 103rd to the 104th, but Contract topics then make up well over half of those hearings in the 104th.

Statistical tests show the differences in committee activity between the 103rd and 104th Congresses to be significant. Table 6 shows the difference of proportions of Contract-topic committee hearings between the 103rd (1993–94) and 104th (1995–96) Congresses. The 104th Congress saw significant increases in the proportion of committee hearings on Contract issues, and this difference appears

Table 6 Difference of proportions tests on Contract-topic legislative activity, 103rd–105th Congresses

	103rd Congress (1993–94)	104th Congress (1995–96)	105th Congress (1997–98)
All hearings, major topic	0.38 (2126)	0.47 (1581)***	0.41 (1709)**
All hearings, subtopic	0.09 (2126)	0.13 (1581)***	0.10 (1709)**
Full hearings, major topic	0.55 (250)	0.56 (335)	0.45 (302)
Full hearings, subtopic	0.08 (250)	0.13 (335)**	0.10 (302)
Subcomm. hearings, major topic	0.36 (1872)	0.44 (1243)***	0.40 (1401)***
Subcomm. hearings, subtopic	0.09 (1872)	0.13 (1243)***	0.10 (1401)**
Nonreferral hearings, major topic	0.38 (1618)	0.45 (1303)***	0.39 (1384)
Nonreferral hearings, subtopic	0.08 (1618)	0.12 (1303)***	0.09 (1384)*
Referral hearings, major topic	0.38 (508)	0.55 (278)***	0.50 (325)***
Referral hearings, subtopic	0.11 (508)	0.18 (278)**	0.14 (325)*
Roll calls, major topic	0.56 (1004)	0.60 (1263)**	0.55 (1070)
Roll calls, subtopic	0.13 (1004)	0.27 (1263)***	0.19 (1070)***
Bill passage roll calls, major topic	0.50 (107)	0.67 (130)***	0.48 (124)
Bill passage roll calls, subtopic	0.07 (107)	0.24 (130)***	0.16 (124)**

Significance tests compare proportions in the 104th or 105th Congress with the 103rd.

N of cases in category in parentheses.

***$p < 0.01$, **$p < 0.05$, *$p < 0.10$, one-tailed tests

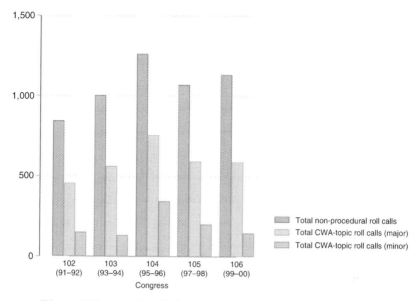

Figure 5 House roll calls by Congress and Contract-topic coding

at several levels. Both referral and nonreferral committee hearings increased on Contract issues (major topic and subtopic), and the proportion of Contract issues increased significantly at the subcommittee level (major and subtopic) and the full-committee level (subtopic only). The Republican-controlled committee system of the 104th Congress turned substantially in the direction of the issues set out in the Contract with America.

On the House floor, the 104th Congress devoted much more attention to Contract topics compared with the Congresses immediately before and after. In contrast to the decline in committee hearings, overall roll-call activity was way up in the new Republican Congress, and Contract-related votes increased, quite disproportionately so among the subtopic Contract issues.[67] Attention to Contract subtopics more than doubled as a proportion from the 103rd to the 104th, as Figure 5 shows. This difference is statistically significant (see Table 6), as is the smaller increase in major-topic Contract issue proportions. And the same significant effect appears when roll calls on passage only are compared.[68] Overall, the size and significance of the increase in legislative activity illustrates a general shift in attention toward the topics the party committed to in the Contract.

To what extent did these agenda shifts endure beyond the first Congress after the election? Figure 4 suggests that Contract-topic committee hearings peaked

---

[67] All procedural votes are excluded from the roll-call totals.

[68] Final passage roll-call data with PAP codes are from Crespin and Rohde (2022).

in the 104th Congress as a proportion, but the heightened relative attention to agenda issues continued into the 105th Congress. The last column in Table 6 shows that, compared with the 104th Congress, the 105th saw smaller but still statistically significant increases in agenda committee attention overall relative to the pre-1994-election 103rd Congress. However, the size of the shift from the 103rd is smaller for all types of committee hearings in the 105th, and some differences that were significant in the 104th are no longer significant. For roll-call votes, Figure 5 shows that floor attention to agenda topics also declined after their peak in the 104th Congress. The comparisons in Table 6 show that major-agenda-topic roll calls were back to roughly their 103rd Congress proportions, though at the subtopic level the 105th Congress still gave slightly more floor attention to the agenda. Overall, the 104th Congress saw a pronounced shift in attention to the Contract agenda in committee and on the floor; that change began to fade but was still detectable in some 105th Congress activity.

3.4 Major Legislative Outcomes and the Contract

The Republican majority made House action on a small number of Contract legislative vehicles the top priority for the first few months of the 104th Congress (Green and Crouch 2022, 126–127). The press paid close attention to the Contract's progress,[69] and according to one observer, "the phrase 'it's in the Contract' came to drive the GOP steamroller in the first 100 days" of the new Congress (Stid 1996, 8). What were the Contract's consequences for specific legislative and public policy outcomes? The evidence is mixed. The new House majority passed measures on nearly all of its Contract priorities, but many of those priorities were never enacted into law. And from a different perspective, most of the major legislative accomplishments of the 104th Congress were non-Contract items.

Republicans brought all Contract items to the floor in 1995, sometimes in legislative form resembling the model Contract legislation, and other times in smaller pieces. Table 7 summarizes specific Contract-focused bills that reached the floor, based on the Republican Conference's own running account of legislative action on the Contract.[70] As others have documented based either on individual bills (Bader 1996, 263–267; Gimpel 1996, 152–153) or on agenda-item summaries

---

[69] See, for example, "'We're ... Halfway Done': Tougher Tests for House Republican 'Contract' Lie Ahead," *Washington Post*, February 20, 1995.

[70] House Republican Conference, Enactment of the Bills of the Contract with America: An Update, September 23, 1997, Gingrich Papers, Box 2132, Folder: Contract with America. The table information is based on the Contract-related bills indicated in the Conference document, with subsequent legislative history filled in based on Congress.gov information. In cases where the House passed both early showcase/catch-all bills and overlapping bills advancing specific policies, the table includes the policy-specific legislative vehicles. Thus, the measures listed in the table represent distinct rather than redundant Contract actions.

Table 7 Contract with America legislation considered on the House floor, 104th Congress

Contract issue	Measure	House passage	Senate passage	Public law[71]
Congressional reform	HR 1[72]	Y	Y	Y
Term limits	HJ Res 73	N	N	N
Fiscal responsibility	HJ Res 1	Y	N	N
	HR 2	Y	Y	Y
National security	HR 7	Y	N	N
Jobs/wages/ regulations	HR 5	Y	Y	Y
	HR 830	Y	Y	Y
	HR 926	Y	N	In part (HR 3136)
	HR 1022	Y	N	N
	HR 925	Y	N	N
Legal reform	HR 956	Y	Y	N
	HR 988	Y	N	N
	HR 1058	Y	Y	Y
Welfare	HR 4	Y	Y	In part (HR 3734)
Tax cut	HR 1215[73]	Y	N	In part (HR 3448, HR 3136, HR 3103)
Social security/ seniors	HR 660	Y	Y	Y
Families	HR 1240	Y	Y	Y
	HR 1271	Y	N	N
Crime	HR 665	Y	Y	In part (S 735)
	HR 666	Y	N	N

[71] Bills are noted as becoming public law if the House bill *or* a Senate version was signed by the president before the end of the 104th Congress. "In part" designation indicates that portions of the House measure were later incorporated into other enacted legislation, per the 1997 House Republican document.

[72] The Contract's congressional reforms were enacted in the Congressional Accountability Act (HR 1) and through a series of House rules changes passed by House resolution in January 1995.

[73] The Republican Conference document treats HR 1215 as part of House action on four Contract categories: Jobs, tax cuts, seniors, and families. HR 1215 passed only in the House. Portions of its jobs/tax policies reached the president's desk as HR 2491, which was vetoed, and several elements were ultimately enacted in other bills as noted in the table.

Table 7 (cont.)

Contract issue	Measure	House passage	Senate passage	Public law
	HR 667	Y	N	In part (HR 3015)
	HR 668	Y	Y (in S 735)	Y (in S 735)
	HR 728	Y	Y (in HR 3019)	Y (in HR 3019)
	HR 729	Y	Y (in S 735)	Y (in S 735)

Sources: House Republican Conference, "Enactment of the Bills of the Contract with America," September, 23, 1997; Congress.gov legislative histories

(Strahan 2007, 166–167), the House cleared all of the Contract items, with the exception of the congressional term limits constitutional amendment. While Republicans could (and did) claim to have kept their promises, the Contract "steamroller" was not as successful in forcing priorities into law. Of the twenty-four separate measures, only ten were signed into law in some form (including Senate alternatives and as later amendments to other bills). The Republican Conference also claimed credit for some elements of five more House Contract bills being included in other legislation in the 104th Congress. House Republicans got nowhere close to enacting all of their priorities, and given internal GOP divisions, Senate differences, and a Democratic president, the enacted measures often stood at some distance from the original Contract legislation (welfare reform is a prominent example of this). Under these constraints, though, the Contract's success in shaping some policy outcomes should not be dismissed.

Yet the Contract's impact on outcomes seems more constrained from the perspective of major legislative accomplishments in the 104th Congress. David Mayhew's list of important enactments from 1995–96 includes fifteen items, the most of the five Congresses in the 1990s (Mayhew 2005). The list features several familiar and consequential laws, such as the Telecommunications Act of 1996, and the Health Insurance Portability and Accountability Act (HIPAA). Only five of the fifteen important enactments are core Contract items (see Table 8), though later in the 104th Congress, Republicans successfully attached provisions from some languishing Contract bills to four additional major enactments. An example is the 1996 minimum wage increase, to which Republicans added some of their business tax cuts. Mayhew has noted that nearly all important outcomes of 1995–96 were passed with strong bipartisan support: fourteen of the fifteen passed with greater than a 2/3 majority in both chambers, and eleven enjoyed majority support from both parties in both chambers (Mayhew 2005, 222–223). The Contract, then helped to shape the

Table 8 Important enactments in the 104th Congress

Title	Contract legislation
Unfunded Mandate Reform Act	Y
Congressional Accountability Act	Y
Lobbying Disclosure Act	N
Private Securities Litigation Reform Act	Y
Personal Responsibility and Work Opportunity Reconciliation Act	Y
Telecommunications Act of 1996	N
Federal Agriculture Improvement and Reform Act of 1996	N
Line Item Veto Act	Y
Antiterrorism and Effective Death Penalty Act	N*
Omnibus Consolidated Rescissions and Appropriations Act (FY96)	N*
Health Insurance Portability and Accountability Act	N*
Small Business Job Protection Act (Minimum wage increase)	N*
Food Quality Protection Act of 1996	N
Safe Drinking Water Act Amendments of 1996	N
Illegal Immigration Reform and Immigrant Responsibility Act (as part of Omnibus Consolidated Appropriations Act, FY97)	N

Note: Important enactments listed in chronological order, based on data from Mayhew (2022); *Indicates enactments that were not Contract-centered, but the GOP claimed they incorporated a provision originally from a Contract bill on final passage.

substantial output of these two congressional sessions, but it was a small part of the 104th Congress' long-term policy impact, and the broad bipartisan backing for the eventual enactments is a reminder that majority-party agenda setting is highly constrained (Curry and Lee 2020).

We can get a sense for the Contract agenda's longer-term impact on legislative priorities through the important enactments in the second Republican Congress (105th, 1997–98). Mayhew identifies only eight important measures from these two sessions (full list available in the Online Appendix). Only one item was clearly Contract-related: ratification of NATO expansion by the Senate in 1998.[74] While Contract items made up

---

[74] A second enactment on Mayhew's list addresses adoption, a component of the Contract's families agenda, but the focus of the 1997 adoption bill differed from the Contract's policy prescription.

a limited but notable part of the 104th's enactments, nearly all of the 105th Congress' major actions were focused on other policy priorities.

3.5 Epilogue: GOP Agendas in the Contract's Aftermath

The Contract with America had a short-term effect on the House and congressional politics, driving general legislative attention and focused work on agenda-related items in the 104th Congress. It had a lingering, less obvious effect on the Republican majority in the later months of the 104th Congress and into the 105th Congress (1997–98). On one hand, Republican members seemed to hold expectations that the leadership would bring the same laser-like focus and energy to House lawmaking after the initial 1995 push for the Contract items. At the same time, many members were unhappy with the intensely centralized process that the leadership followed in the 104th Congress (Strahan 2007). And, in the wake of Contract-centered legislating in 1995, House committees and outside groups had long wish lists of items outside of the Contract that they hoped to move to the forefront. What followed was a more inwardly directed process of agenda formation with the Contract as backdrop, as congressional Republicans did not successfully formulate a major public campaign agenda again in the 1990s.

As early as January 1996, one year after the Republicans took the majority, Republican leaders were working to develop a plan for both legislation and messaging in the second half of the 104th Congress. A plan draft explained that "House Republicans saw the most success during the first 100 days when they were following a carefully developed plan," and a related memo noted that "the sense of purpose that prevailed in the Contract period has evaporated"[75] Majority staff explored a huge range of issue options for the second session, ranging from Medicaid reform to the elimination of the Commerce Department. The staff analyses highlighted concerns with targeting key voting blocs, such as Ross Perot voters, that had been part of the Contract's development, but they also showed concern with developing "rifle shot" issues that would "energize our coalition."[76] House Republicans eventually settled on a short list of broad issue areas, overlapping with the Contract, for their second year in the majority: "Drug enforcement, illegal immigration, the economy, welfare reform, and presidential ethics" (Green and Crouch 2022, 136). The early 1996 planning illustrates the struggle of a House majority initially animated by a relatively limited electoral agenda, now searching for a new focus.

---

[75] House GOP Conference Preliminary Strategic and Operational Plan for 1996, January 22, 1996, and Preliminary Recommendations of Majority Planning Group/Planning Systems Team, January 19, 1996, Tom DeLay Papers, University of Houston Libraries Special Collections, Box 99, Folder 39.

[76] Various staff memos, February 15, 1996, DeLay Papers, Box 99, Folder 39.

For the next Congress, House Republicans did not follow their 1994 model; instead they turned to agenda-making *after* the 1996 election, working internally on an agenda that might bring Contract-like legislative focus for the 105th Congress while avoiding some of its pitfalls. Just before the election, Majority Leader Dick Armey's staff set out plans for a somewhat more committee-centered process in 1997, and envisioned a limited legislative and communications agenda that was "not as broad as a Contract II-type commitment." House committees had also advanced long lists of priorities for 1997, most of which veered from the Contract topics,[77] and at the start of the new Congress, Armey's office was also collecting the many priorities of Republican-aligned outside groups, including the Christian Coalition, the National Rifle Association, and the Eagle Forum.[78]

The conference moved slowly toward a formal agenda in the early months of 1997. Member meetings in February yielded "a consensus" on the party's "highest legislative priorities,"[79] but it took until March before the leadership released a final agenda. Meanwhile, Armey sent a somewhat apologetic message to the conference, noting that many members "appear disappointed that the 105th Congress hasn't started out with the legislative whirlwind of the 104th," and promising that "the floor schedule will build to a crescendo of progress" as committees worked on agenda-related legislation.[80] When the "Creating a Better America" agenda arrived in March, it identified twelve priorities and associated legislative action items, with some building on unfinished Contract business but others launching in different directions.[81] House Republicans made little progress on the agenda in the 105th Congress amidst internal controversies, Gingrich's declining influence and strategic missteps (Green and Crouch 2022, 152), and the White House scandal (Rae and Campbell 1999, 7–9), but their effort to structure the agenda illustrated the persistent appeal of Contract-style focus within the conference.[82]

---

[77] Peter [Davidson] to Dick [Armey] and Kerry [Knott], October 31, 1996, Dick Armey Collection, Carl Albert Center, University of Oklahoma, Series 12, Box 55, Folder 12.

[78] Coalitions Report, January 1997, Armey Collection, Series 12, Box 55, Folder 13.

[79] John Boehner, Susan Molinari, and Jennifer Dunn to Republican Colleague, February 8, 1997, Armey Collection, Series 12, Box 55, Folder 13.

[80] Dick Armey to Republican members, February 26, 1997, Armey Collection, Series 12, Box 55, Folder 13.

[81] Peter Davidson to John Sampson, March 4, 1997, and "Better America" agenda, March 6, 1997, Armey Collection, series 12, Box 55, Folder 14.

[82] A last attempt at House Republican agenda-making in the Clinton era emerged from a failed Gingrich initiative before the 1998 election. In spring 1998, Gingrich developed a "Goals for a Generation" agenda, along with a fairly elaborate plan for publicity of its four broad goals. Unlike the 1997 agenda, Goals for a Generation was pitched with Contract-style public promises. Although press coverage suggests Gingrich himself spoke frequently about the agenda in mid-1998 – and made it

3.6 Contract with America: Summary

The 1994 Contract with America emerged from House Republicans' strategic choice, under Newt Gingrich's leadership, to define a concise policy agenda that could both achieve substantial support in the conference and target conservative voters. The Contract's internal development illustrates a substantial role for the leadership but also considerable participation by members and even candidates in shaping its content. That content, in turn, corresponded disproportionately with the revealed issue priorities of more conservative House Republicans in individual bill introductions in the two years leading up to the 1994 election. In that same time frame, Republican minority-party leaders were using tools at their disposal to emphasize the issues that would eventually become part of the Contract's promises. Republicans as a group were far more likely to center their floor speeches on the issue areas that ultimately went into the Contract, and it was more junior Republicans and top GOP leaders, who were individually more likely to speak on those issues. The leadership further demonstrated its emphasis on Contract topics in motions to recommit.

The Contract then foreshadowed House legislative activity in the 104th Congress in several respects. The majority's turn toward its issues extended beyond a few key pieces of legislation – committee hearings and floor votes shifted significantly in the direction of Contract topics. Republicans successfully moved nearly all of their designated Contract bills through the House, but saw only mixed success in enacting those priorities and in shaping the direction of major enactments. Finally, the Contract's aftereffects continued for House Republicans over the next several years, as members sought the focus that came from a defined issue agenda but the leadership grappled with the pent-up demand for action on many other priorities from outside groups and from their own committees.

4 Democrats: The 2006 New Direction for America

4.1 Origins

The 2006 midterm elections offered an unusually promising opportunity for Democrats, who had been in the House minority since 1995. President George W. Bush's approval ratings hovered in the 30s through the year as the unpopular

---

central to his book tour that year – the agenda seems to have been lost in the chaos of that year's politics. "Goals for a Generation" draft plan, March 16, 1998, Gingrich Papers, Box 2433, Folder: Goals for a Generation; House Republican Communications Playbook, August 1998, Gingrich Papers, Box 2436, Folder: House Republican Communications Playbook. On Gingrich's promotion of the agenda and his book, see Juliet Eilperin, "The Education of Newt Gingrich," *Washington Post*, April 7, 1998.

Iraq War continued and the Hurricane Katrina crisis cast Bush's leadership in a negative light. After a particularly successful recruitment season in swing districts, the Democrats picked up thirty seats (and the majority) in the House, and just enough Senate seats for a fifty-one-vote majority with the two Democratic-caucusing independents. As with Republicans in 1994, Democrats planned an election-year agenda effort in 2006, formally titled "A New Direction for America," and often referred to as "Six for '06." The shorthand title referred to a series of six broad agenda priorities –real security, prosperity, opportunity, energy independence, affordable health care, and retirement security and dignity– with associated specific policy items.[83]

Democratic congressional leaders began early in the 2006 election cycle to develop a set of issue statements. In February 2005, Minority Leader Nancy Pelosi released a "Plan for Jobs and Prosperity" that included early versions of the minimum wage and energy proposals that later appeared in the New Direction agenda.[84] As the 109th Congress proceeded, House Democrats coordinated with the Senate Democratic leadership, and they used a participatory process that was inclusive of different segments of the Democratic Caucus.[85] Other components of the eventual New Direction proposals appeared over time, including the "Plan for Real Security," focused on terrorism and the Iraq War, in March 2006.[86]

As was the case with the Republicans in 1994, negotiations on the Democratic agenda in 2006 were sometimes contentious: George Miller (D-CA) said that "it threatened to come apart, then it would come together, then it would threaten to come apart" (Bendavid 2007, 141). Reporting on the process emphasized that the caucus steered away from "traditionally liberal ideas like universal health care" in building support,[87] and set aside other contentious items such as a reversal of the 2001–03 Bush tax cuts.[88] With the final choice of these fairly centrist priorities, more progressive members were left unsatisfied: They "found the message effort underdeveloped and too vacuous, far short of a governing philosophy and lacking a clear embrace of stances they wanted such as a commitment to end the Iraq War, a fix of the alternative

---

[83] "A New Direction for America," September 1, 2006, HouseDemocrats.gov via archive.org, July 4, 2019. web.archive.org/web/20061129202443/ http://www.democraticleader.house.gov /pdf/thebook.pdf.

[84] "A Plan for Jobs and Prosperity: The New Partnership for America's Future," February 16, 2005, David Obey Papers, University of Wisconsin – Stevens Point Archives, Box 889, Folder 5.

[85] Jeffrey H. Birnbaum and Jonathan Weisman, "House Democrats Propose More Spending for Military and Education," *Washington Post*, November 1, 2006.

[86] Press release, March 29, 2006, Obey Papers, Box 889, Folder 9.

[87] Kate Zernike, "Ready to Be the Voice of the Majority," *New York Times*, November 9, 2006.

[88] Birnbaum and Weisman, "House Democrats Propose More Spending for Military and Education."

minimum tax, and progress on poverty and economic inequality" (Peters and Rosenthal 2010, 138–140). In the choice of issue *framing*, though, Nancy Pelosi and other Democratic leaders were accommodating more progressive, "netroots" Democrats (Peters and Rosenthal 2010, 136–137). The resulting New Direction document was narrowly focused in its issue priorities and carefully framed in drawing issue contrasts with the incumbent Republican government.[89]

Democrats first presented the full six-item New Direction for America agenda in mid-June 2006, and began a summer messaging focus on the individual items in the agenda.[90] House leaders urged Democrats during the July recess "to hold at least one district event ... on the priorities in the Democrats' New Direction for America," and they continued to press members to promote the agenda during the summer, including by featuring agenda materials on member websites.[91] In mid-July, House Democrats held a conference for staff on the agenda. Attendees heard from Democratic pollsters Celinda Lake and Cornell Belcher about message polling on the agenda, and from committee, leadership, and member staffers about plans for "message implementation," along with a keynote from former DNC chair Terry McAuliffe.[92] The DNC itself was involved in coordinating a late-July national organizing day of canvassing and events centered on the New Direction themes.[93]

The June agenda focused on top-line priorities. Then, in September, the party unveiled a more detailed version of the agenda, in the form of a thirty-one-page document that elaborated on the six priorities. That document also appended a section on "Honest Leadership and Open Government" that addressed Washington procedural reforms, including lobbying rules, "regular order" in the House, and pay-as-you-go budgeting requirements.[94] Democrats then identified a small set of key items from the larger New Direction plan for a first-100-hours agenda, setting aside some low-hanging fruit from the more extensive document.[95] This 100-hours list was designed to attract some bipartisan support and thereby communicate a positive governing message

---

[89] Carl Hulse, "Should They Win Control of Congress, the Democrats Have a Plan," *New York Times*, November 4, 2006. Bendavid (2007, 141) suggests that the party was fixed very early on limiting the agenda to six items.

[90] David Nather, "Dems Strike Out Haltingly in 'New Direction,'" *CQ Weekly*, July 31, 2006.

[91] Nancy Pelosi, Steny Hoyer, and James Clyburn to Democratic Colleague, June 22, 2006, Obey Papers, Box 889, Folder 9; Mary Ann Akers, "Heard on the Hill," *Roll Call*, September 21, 2006.

[92] 2006 Democratic Caucus Staff Issues Conference agenda, July 17, 2006, Obey Papers, Box 889, Folder 9.

[93] Howard Dean to Member of Congress, July 11, 2006, Obey Papers, Box 889, Folder 9.

[94] "A New Direction for America," September 1, 2006, HouseDemocrats.gov via archive.org, July 4, 2019. web.archive.org/web/20061129202443/ http://www.democraticleader.house.gov/pdf/thebook.pdf.

[95] Office of Speaker-Designate Nancy Pelosi, Overview Packet on the "100 Hours" Legislation, December 8, 2006, Obey Papers, Box 889, Folder 9.

(Sinclair 2008). Appropriations Committee chair David Obey (D-WI) referred to these promises as "modest proposals" that "set the stage" for bigger priorities like health care reform.[96]

As a messaging effort, the New Direction was fairly successful. Democratic leaders adhered to the messaging language through 2006 and into the new Congress.[97] Like the 1994 Contract, the agenda broke through in press coverage during the election, in postelection interpretation, and as the new Congress began its work.[98] For instance, an early November *New York Times* headline stated "Should They Win Control of Congress, the Democrats Have a Plan."[99] At the same time, and again like the Contract, there is no clear evidence that the New Direction for America had a direct, measurable impact on voters.[100] The agenda, overall, was driven by leadership decisions with participation by rank-and-file members, and it reflected a selective, strategic approach to campaign promises. In one important contrast with the Contract, the New Direction was rolled out earlier and in stages, with the leadership presenting some elements more than a year before the election, and offering more details as the election season began in earnest.

4.2 Whose Issue Priorities?

As in Section 3 on the Contract with America, I connect the issues in the 2006 New Direction to the demonstrated member and leadership priorities within the party. Bill introduction data capture the revealed issue priorities of individual members, and motions to recommit and floor speeches show where the minority-party leadership was placing its message emphasis prior to the 2006 election.

4.2.1 Member Priorities: Evidence from Bill Introductions

Issue priorities for members of the Democratic caucus appear in their bill introductions. At the individual level, there is no evidence that the agenda followed from a major surge in Democrats' attention to related priorities in the Congress before the 2006 election (109th). Instead, individual attention to the agenda's items ticked up a bit, at least in the main topic areas, in the two

---

[96] David Obey, "Providing a New Direction for America in the First 100 Hours of the New Congress," press release, undated, Obey Papers, Box 889, Folder 10.

[97] Between June 1, 2006 and December 31, 2007, eighty-six *New York Times* articles contained both "new direction" and "Democrats," with "new direction" typically being used by Democratic leaders.

[98] As was the case with the Contract, some reporting and commentary was deeply skeptical. See Steven Perlstein, "Democrats May Be Poised to Win, but They're Still Lost," *Washington Post*, October 25, 2006; Michael Kinsley, "Pelosi's Platform," *Washington Post*, November 7, 2006.

[99] *New York Times*, November 4, 2006.

[100] Adam Nagourney, "1994, the Election to Embrace (and Avoid)," *New York Times*, September 24, 2006.

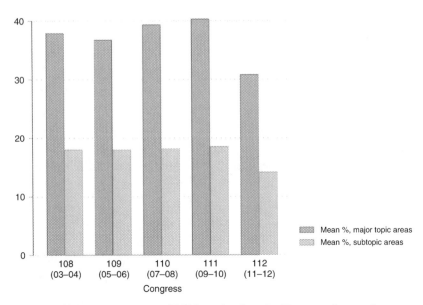

Figure 6 Mean percentage of bill introductions by Democratic members on
New Direction topics

Congresses after the Democrats took the majority, as Figure 6 shows. The data
in Figure 7 put this finding in context: overall bill introduction activity among
Democrats shot up in the two Democratic-majority Congresses (110th & 111th),
and the raw numbers of introductions in agenda main topics and subtopics also
increased substantially. As a proportion of total bills members introduced on
average, however, there was little change when viewed in the aggregate.

What segments of the Democratic caucus individually prioritized the issues
in the New Direction agenda in the years before the 2006 election? Table 9
presents negative binomial regression models of Democratic bill introductions
on agenda topics (subtopic PAP coding) for the Democratic-minority 109th
Congress (2005–06).[101] Recall that Contract with America content reflected the
bill introduction priorities of more conservative, but not more electorally
marginal members of the Republican caucus in 1993–94.

For the Democrats in the 2006 cycle, the public agenda reflected the priorities
of *electorally vulnerable* Democrats: sponsorship of agenda topics significantly
decreased as vote share increased. Member ideological positioning in the
caucus, as indicated by Nominate score, is not a significant predictor. For
Democrats in the 2000s, vote share and Nominate scores are correlated at

---

[101] When the analysis in Table 9 is conducted using OLS, the results are substantively similar (see
Online Appendix). The bill-introduction models in Table 9 and in the Online Appendix exclude
one extreme outlier on total introductions, Rob Andrews (D-NJ).

Table 9 House Democratic bill introductions on New Direction topics (subtopic PAP coding), 109th Congress

Total impt. bills	0.068***
	(0.007)
DW-Nom. (1st)	−0.569
	(0.429)
Tenure	−0.012
	(0.014)
Top leader	−0.017
	(0.389)
Dem. vote share	−0.012**
	(0.005)
Constant	0.684**
	(0.338)
N	201

Negative binomial regression; standard errors in parentheses.
***$p < 0.01$, **$p < 0.05$

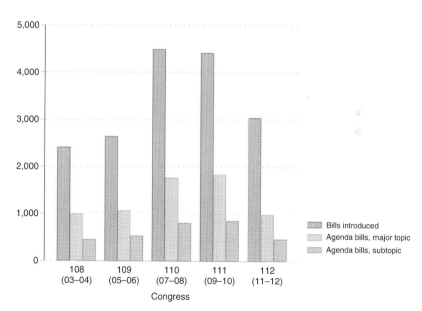

Figure 7 Total bill introductions by Democratic members

moderate levels, so I have repeated the analysis omitting each of those variables. These results (see Online Appendix) confirm the results from the full model.

Overall, the patterns of bill introductions for Democrats suggest that the 2006 agenda spoke to the issue priorities of more marginal members before the election – those members who represented contested swing districts that Democrats needed to seize the House majority.[102] This finding on the agenda's issue emphasis is consistent with what we know about the national challenges facing Democrats in recent decades. The Democratic Party remains a diverse group coalition party (Grossmann and Hopkins 2016), with incentives to appeal to voters on the basis of policy positions that serve group interests rather than ideology. And the geography of American politics in recent decades has required Democrats to compete in more potentially hostile territory. "Returning the party to majority status," Hopkins has argued, has "virtually necessitated winning seats that fundamentally leaned Republican in presidential elections" (2017, 168). As Democrats select a small set of issues for a national congressional agenda, then, we see an emphasis on issues that have demonstrated appeal to members from marginal districts – in contrast to the Republican 1994 strategy of representing conservative priorities.

4.2.2 Party-Coordinated Priorities: Evidence from Floor Speeches

Members' one-minute floor speeches highlight choices over issue emphasis in a public position-taking venue. As discussed in Section 3, one-minute speeches are subject to considerable coordination by party leaders as a messaging tool. Knowing that the New Direction for America reflected Democratic minority-party messaging in the 109th Congress, we would expect to see greater attention to New Direction topics among Democrats in that pre-2006-election Congress. Figure 8 illustrates that Democrats gave considerably fewer one-minute speeches *overall* compared with majority Republicans, but they spoke more about the agenda major-topic areas, both in absolute terms and as a proportion of each party's speeches (27.5% vs. 18.5%, $p < 0.001$).

At the individual level, the negative binomial regression model in Table 10 shows more junior Democrats were significantly more likely to speak on New Direction major topics.[103] However, in contrast to Republicans, whose top leaders were more likely to speak on Contract topics in the 103rd Congress, there is no significant difference between the leadership and rank-and-file for

---

[102] The results in Table 9 are similar when the models use major-topic introductions as the dependent variable. In other words, the electoral marginality effect for Democrats holds for subtopic and major topic agenda items. This result contrasts with the Contract findings for Republicans (Table 2), where the relationship with member conservatism held only for subtopic items.

[103] When analyzed using OLS, this model does not show significant effects for the tenure variable, although the bivariate relationship between tenure and agenda-topic speeches is significant. Because the speeches data is overdispersed count data, I present the negative binomial results here; OLS results are available in the Online Appendix.

Table 10 House Democratic one-minute speeches on
New Direction topics (major-topic PAP coding),
109th Congress

Total speeches	0.080***
	(0.011)
DW-Nom. (1st)	−0.878
	(0.772)
Tenure	−0.084***
	(0.031)
Top leader	−1.037
	(1.105)
Dem. vote share	−0.006
	(0.008)
Constant	0.043
	(0.538)
N	202

Negative binomial regression; standard errors in parentheses
*** $p < 0.01$

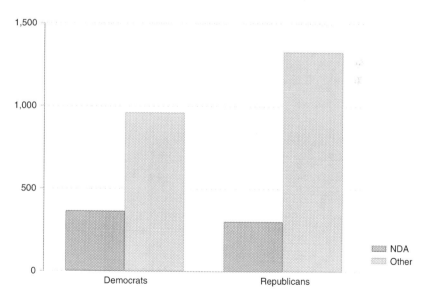

Figure 8 One-minute speeches by party, 109th Congress (2005–06)

Table 11 Motions to recommit and straight amendments
by New Direction major topic, 109th Congress

	Amendment votes	Motions to recommit	Total
Other topic	298	28	326
	72.15%	52.83%	69.96%
New Direction topic	115	25	140
	27.85%	47.17%	30.04%
Total	413	53	466
	100%	100%	100%

Note: $\chi^2 = 8.34$ ($p = 0.004$)

Democrats on the New Direction agenda when total speeches are controlled. In addition, electoral security is unrelated to members' speeches on New Direction topics, in contrast to the patterns for member bill introductions in the same Congress.

4.2.3 Leadership Message Priorities: Evidence from Minority-Party Motions

The minority party's choices over themes in motions to recommit capture the party leadership's decisions about how to use legislative process for public messaging. In 2005–06, the Democratic leadership offered motions to recommit on New Directions topics relatively frequently. The minority's motions to recommit addressed agenda major topics almost half of the time – much more frequently than the appearance of those topics on amendment floor votes (28 percent, see Table 11).[104] A similar pattern appears when motions and amendments in the 109th Congress are broken down by New Direction sub-topics. Table 12 shows that about 28 percent of motions to recommit were on agenda subtopics, compared to about 13 percent of amendment votes. This pattern is consistent with an effort by Democratic leaders to call attention to the New Direction agenda in the legislative process in the Congress leading up to the 2006 election.[105]

---

[104] See Section 3.2 for details on motions and amendment data.
[105] Democrats in the 109th Congress were also significantly more likely than majority Republicans to sponsor floor amendments on New Direction topics and subtopics (see Online Appendix). The proportion of motions to recommit (MTR) on New Direction topics was considerably higher than for floor amendments, however. About 32 percent of Democratic-sponsored amendments were on major New Direction topics (compared with 23 percent for Republicans), compared with 47 percent of MTRs on those topics.

Table 12 Motions to recommit and straight amendments by New Direction subtopic, 109th Congress

	Amendment votes	Motions to recommit	Total
Other subtopic	361 87.41%	38 71.70%	399 85.62%
New Direction subtopic	52 12.59%	15 28.30%	67 14.38%
Total	413 100%	53 100%	466 100%

Note: $\chi^2 = 9.42$ ($p = 0.002$)

4.2.4 Member Responses to the Leadership: Evidence from Agenda Promotion

Additional data available for the 2006 case allow some supplementary analysis about individual members' decisions to promote the New Direction agenda *after* it was formally unveiled. The Democrats' agenda effort lacked the signing ceremony that accompanied the Contract with America, so individual members were not asked to commit publicly to the agenda's priorities in the same way. But the leadership did lean on rank-and-file members to promote the agenda, including by advertising it on their official House websites.[106] We know that legislators are strategic about their online self-presentation (Gulati 2004; Russell 2021), and archived September 2006 member websites provide a rough indicator of which members were ready and willing to advertise the leadership's agenda. I accessed the archived official websites of each incumbent Democrat and coded whether they directly presented the New Direction agenda in some form at the end of September 2006.[107] Overall, just over half of the incumbent Democrats running for reelection (97 out of 191) advertised the agenda on their official website in some form.

---

[106] Akers, "Heard on the Hill."

[107] I used the Internet Archive and the Library of Congress' archive to access all incumbent Democrats' official pages as archived on the latest available date in September 2006 (September 30 in the vast majority of cases). This timing falls after the rollout of the full agenda and squarely in the middle of the fall general election campaign. I coded a member's site as promoting the agenda if their main page, press release page, or issues page contained any New Direction material. Most members who advertised the agenda included a New Direction graphic and link on their home page, sometimes with a brief explanation. Some members went further, including state-specific data on the agenda's priorities, for instance, or crafting other material on their home page around New Direction talking points.

Table 13 House Democrats advertising the 2006 New Direction agenda, 109th Congress

	(1)	(2)	(3)
DW-Nom. (1st)	−4.663***		−5.099***
	(1.236)		(1.204)
Dem. vote share	0.018	0.032**	
	(0.013)	(0.013)	
Top leader	0.325	0.110	0.260
	(1.076)	(1.047)	(1.053)
Tenure	−0.040	−0.020	−0.030
	(0.037)	(0.035)	(0.036)
CBC member	−1.046**	−0.730*	−0.865**
	(0.438)	(0.419)	(0.411)
Constant	−2.792***	−2.009**	−1.790***
	(0.919)	(0.869)	(0.520)
N	191	191	191

Logit coefficients; standard errors in parentheses.
***$p < 0.01$, **$p < 0.05$, *$p < 0.10$

I use this indicator as a dependent variable in logit models in Table 13 as I seek to identify which Democrats in 2006 were more likely to advertise the agenda. These models include the independent variables used to predict agenda-related bill introductions, as well as a control for Congressional Black Caucus (CBC) membership since CBC Democrats appeared particularly unlikely to advertise the Democratic leadership's agenda package.[108] Because of moderate collinearity between Nominate scores and Democratic vote share, Table 13 presents a full model as well as models removing the Nominate and vote share variables. The results add an important piece to the story: Democrats who associated themselves with the leadership's agenda were, on average, more electorally secure and more liberal incumbents. In other words, the Democrats crafted an agenda that emphasized the concerns of their more vulnerable incumbents – the members who represented the types of districts that Democrats hoped to take over in November. But the members who were most likely to respond to the leadership's push to promote the agenda were not those whose issue priorities were embodied in the agenda.

---

[108] Sixteen of thirty-six CBC members advertised the agenda, although CBC members were significantly more liberal and electorally secure than other Democrats. Still, excluding this variable does not change the substantive conclusions from the Table 13 models.

4.2.5 New Direction Priorities: Summary

The quantitative evidence on New Direction for America issues tells a story that distinguishes between the source of strategic agenda priorities and the party and individual decisions to *promote* the agenda. In bill sponsorship activity prior to the 2006 election, individual Democrats who were more electorally vulnerable gave significantly more attention to New Direction issues – this finding is consistent with the process evidence that suggests Democratic leaders crafted an agenda to appeal to swing voters in competitive districts. The minority party showed substantial attention to this set of issues in one-minute floor speeches and in motions to recommit in the 109th Congress. This picture of a leadership-promoted agenda designed to favor vulnerable members' priorities is enhanced by the evidence on members' decisions to promote the agenda in the fall. Although the priorities favored marginal Democrats, the members eager to sell the national message that the leadership had been emphasizing were the more ideologically extreme and electorally secure.

4.3 Consequences for Legislative Activity

After the Democrats took the majority in the 2006 election, the leadership shifted Congress' attention in committee and on the House floor toward New Direction for America issue priorities. Committee hearing activity was up substantially in the 110th Congress (2007–08), as Figure 9 shows, and

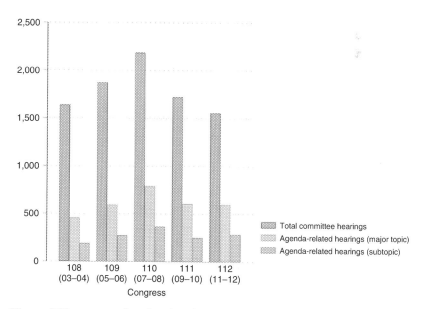

Figure 9 House committee hearings by Congress and New Direction topic coding

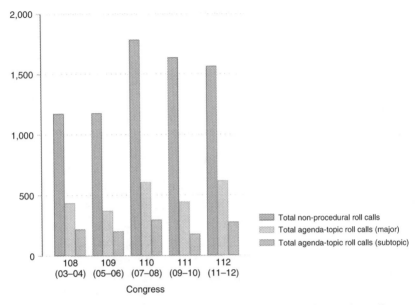

Figure 10 House roll calls by Congress and New Direction topic coding

hearings on agenda topics were up even as a proportion of the rising overall number of hearings. This attention is particular to the 110th Congress, since hearings and attention to agenda topics fell back somewhat in the 111th Congress. The increases in the proportion of agenda-topic-related hearings are statistically significant in the 110th Congress for both major and subtopic hearings, as Table 14 shows. Significant differences appear in the 110th Congress across both referral and nonreferral hearings (both major topic and subtopic). Dividing hearings by subcommittee and full-committee hearings shows that the increases in agenda topic hearings at the subcommittee level were significant, although the small increases in agenda related full-committee hearings did not rise to significant levels.

Just as the change of party control in the 104th Congress saw a burst of floor activity, the switch back to Democratic control in the 110th led to a sharp rise in floor votes (Figure 10). The total number of New Direction topic floor votes is the highest in the 110th, in absolute terms, of the 108th–112th Congresses. And attention to agenda topics as a proportion of all nonprocedural votes was much higher, particularly for major-topic votes, in this first Democratic-controlled House than in the Republican 109th House (see Table 14). Note, though, that there are not significant differences when the small numbers of final passage votes are compared. Overall, both committee hearings and floor attention highlight the party's considerably greater focus on agenda-related legislative activity in the first Congress after the 2006 campaign.

Table 14 Difference of proportions tests on New Direction topic legislative activity, 109th–111th Congresses

	109th Congress (2005–06)	110th Congress (2007–08)	111th Congress (2009–10)
All hearings, major topic	0.32 (1872)	0.36 (2188)***	0.35 (1737)**
All hearings, subtopic	0.15 (1872)	0.17 (2188)**	0.14 (1737)
Full hearings, major topic	0.38 (525)	0.40 (664)	0.40 (493)
Full hearings, subtopic	0.17 (525)	0.18 (664)	0.15 (493)
Subcomm. hearings, major topic	0.29 (1347)	0.35 (1523)***	0.33 (1239)**
Subcomm. hearings, subtopic	0.14 (1347)	0.16 (1523)**	0.14 (1239)
Nonreferral hearings, major topic	0.34 (1635)	0.38 (1879)**	0.36 (1518)*
Nonreferral hearings, subtopic	0.15 (1635)	0.17 (1879)*	0.15 (1518)
Referral hearings, major topic	0.17 (237)	0.28 (309)***	0.26 (219)***
Referral hearings, subtopic	0.08 (237)	0.13 (309)*	0.11 (219)
Roll calls, major topic	0.31 (1194)	0.34 (1787)**	0.27 (1639)
Roll calls, subtopic	0.17 (1194)	0.17 (1787)	0.11 (1639)
Bill passage roll calls, major topic	0.37 (119)	0.36 (149)	0.30 (104)
Bill passage roll calls, subtopic	0.24 (119)	0.20 (149)	0.12 (104)

Significance tests compare proportions in the 110th or 111th Congress with the 109th.

N of cases in category in parentheses.

***$p < 0.01$, **$p < 0.05$, *$p < 0.10$, one-tailed tests

Some of the spike in agenda attention lingered into the second Congress after the election (111th). At the committee level, the proportion of hearings on major New Direction topics remained significantly higher into the 111th Congress, as Figure 9 and the last column in Table 14 show. At the subtopic level, however, attention reverted back to about the same levels as in the 109th Congress. The limited uptick in floor voting attention in the postelection 110th Congress did not continue into the 111th, with New Direction topics receiving slightly less relative attention than they did before the 2006 election. As the Contract with America also showed, some agenda effects lingered into the second Congress after the New Direction agenda, but the shift in attention was fading rapidly after the 110th Congress.

4.4 Major Legislative Outcomes and the New Direction

At the start of the new 110th Congress, Democrats focused on a few key legislative actions that showcased the New Direction for America agenda, moving an initial set of measures through the House in the first 100 hours.[109] These items included six agenda-focused bills (numbered HR 1 through HR 6), as well as House rules changes that enacted some of the promises about ethics and budgeting reforms that had been appended to the New Direction document.[110] Democratic leaders were eager to explain that these early actions were only a first step in action on the agenda, and that the regular order for legislation that they had pledged would begin after the initial round of bills cleared the House – and to advertise the substantial Republican support that the 100-hours measures received.[111]

As the 110th Congress proceeded, Democratic leaders tried to keep the focus on the New Direction theme, often blurring advertising of unrelated congressional actions with the agenda itself.[112] Speaker Pelosi marked the one-year anniversary of the Democrats' 2006 victory with a Capitol-steps event heralding the "remarkable record of progress" on New Direction topics and other issues.[113] As with the Republicans' Contract, we should ask what the record looks like in terms of measures enacted, as well as the relative contribution the New Direction agenda made to major legislative accomplishments in the 110th Congress.

---

[109] "Manifesto for the First 100 Hours," *CQ Weekly*, November 20, 2006.

[110] "In its First 100 Hours, New Congress Provides a New Direction for America," press release, undated, Obey Papers, Box 889, Folder 9.

[111] "Questions & Answers on the '100 Hours' Bills," and "100 Hours Agenda Passes with Bipartisan Support," Obey Papers, Box 889, Folder 9.

[112] "A Five-Month Progress Report: House Democrats are Moving America in a New Direction," Office of Majority Leader Steny Hoyer, May 22, 2007, Obey Papers, Box 889, Folder 10.

[113] Nancy Pelosi, New Direction event announcement, October 29, 2007, and "The 110th Congress: A New Direction for America," undated, Obey Papers, Box 889, Folder 9.

Table 15 New Direction for America legislation considered on the House floor, 110th Congress

New Direction issue	Measure	House passage	Senate passage	Public law
Real security	HR 1	Y	Y	Y
	HR 1591	Y	Y	N
	HR 2764	Y	Y	Y
	S 22	Y	Y	Y (in HR 2642)
	HR 4986	Y	Y	Y
Jobs/pay	HR 2	Y	Y	Y (in HR 2206)
	HR 2272	Y	Y	Y
	HR 6049	Y	Y	N
College access	HR 2669	Y	Y	Y
Energy/gas prices	HR 6	Y	Y	Y (combined with HR 3221 and HR 2776)
	HR 6074	Y	N	N
Drug costs/stem cells	S 5	Y	Y	N
	HR 4	Y	N	N
Retirement security	none			

Sources: *CQ Weekly* (various editions); Obey Papers, Box 889, Folder 9; Speaker's office press releases (various dates); Congress.gov

Table 15 summarizes action on agenda-connected items that reached the House floor in the 110th Congress.[114] Democrats brought measures on nearly all main promises in the agenda to a House vote in 2007. The first agenda item (a minimum wage increase) was signed into law in the spring, and Democrats could claim credit for several more, including enactment of the 9/11 Commission's recommendations and a student loan and Pell grant reform bill,

---

[114] Tracking action on agenda items in the 110th is more challenging than for the 104th since a retrospective from the caucus on agenda-specific action is not available. Press documents from the Speaker's office (in the Obey papers and on the archived Speaker's website) identify a wide range of "New Direction" accomplishments that are not related to the specific agenda promises. To identify the measures in Table 15, I used a broad list of 110th Congress actions on the Speaker's website from late 2008 (https://web.archive.org/web/20090103050609/ www .speaker.gov/newsroom/reports?id=0074) as well as *CQ Weekly*'s annual legislative summaries to identify major initiatives on the promises specifically included in the New Direction, and I traced legislative histories of these measures on Congress.gov. Several agenda promises were the subject of multiple measures on the House floor, and the table includes the vehicle that progressed the farthest toward enactment in those cases.

by the year's end.[115] But with a Senate only narrowly controlled by Democrats and a Republican in the White House, Democrats faced a tougher task on many other items. Legislation on issues like drug costs, stem cell research funding, and – most prominently – the Iraq War either faced a presidential veto or could not pass both chambers in 2007.[116] Still, several more important items from the agenda cleared the president's desk in some form in late 2007 or 2008, including a compromise version of the New Direction's energy priorities and elements of a new GI college bill. Most of the Democrats' attention to the agenda was confined to the first session. By the second session, the press of other issues, particularly the housing and financial crises, dominated Congress' work.

It is notable that one important component of the 2006 agenda received no major attention from Democrats in the 110th Congress – retirement security. This plank of the New Direction agenda centered on a negative promise to "stop any plan to privatize Social Security," a reaction to President Bush's failed initiative from 2005. Although the agenda also committed to pension-plan reform and incentives for personal savings, Democrats did not act on retirement plans and Social Security.

Through the lens of the 110th Congress' major enactments, the Democrats' agenda impact is modest but discernable. Table 16 lists Mayhew's important legislative actions from 2007 and 2008 (Mayhew 2022). These fifteen laws include five separate New Direction agenda measures, plus the major lobbying reform bill that Democrats had discussed alongside the main agenda. The pattern here is similar to the Contract's impact on the 104th Congress: the major enactments at the start of the 110th Congress are bipartisan or compromise bills that emerged from the new majority's agenda, but other agenda-setting factors moved Washington quickly beyond the low-hanging fruit from the 2006 election agenda. In the 111th Congress (2009–10), major enactments continued to follow the pressures of the changing political and economic context, but two of the sixteen measures on Mayhew's list were closely related to original commitments in the 2006 agenda – further student loan and Pell grant reforms (in the Affordable Care Act reconciliation bill) and support for 9/11 responders.[117]

---

[115] Stephen Labaton, "Congress Passes Increase in Minimum Wage," *New York Times*, May 25, 2007; David Herszenhorn, "Congress Averts Higher Tax Bill for the Middle Class," *New York Times*, December 20, 2007.

[116] Clive Crook, "Victorious Democrats' Big Ideas Yielded Small Results," *Financial Times*, December 24, 2007; Carl Hulse and Robert Pear, "Republican Unity Trumps Democratic Momentum," *New York Times*, December 21, 2007; Richard Simon and Noam N. Levey, "Democrats Savor Power for a Year but End It Feeling Unfulfilled," *Los Angeles Times*, December 20, 2007.

[117] Full list of 111th Congress major enactments is available in the Online Appendix.

Table 16 Important enactments in the 110th Congress

Title	New Direction legislation
Fair Minimum Wage Act (in 2007 supplemental appropriations)	Y
Implementing Recommendations of the 9/11 Commission Act	Y
Honest Leadership and Open Government Act (HLOGA)	N*
College Cost Reduction and Access Act	Y
Energy Independence and Security Act	Y
Economic Stimulus Act of 2008	N
Post-9/11 Veterans Educational Assistance Act (modified, in 2008 supplemental appropriations)	Y
Food, Conservation, and Energy Act	N
Housing and Economic Recovery Act of 2008	N
FISA Amendments Act	N
Emergency Economic Stabilization Act	N
Mental Health Parity and Addiction Equity Act (in Emergency Economic Stabilization Act)	N
United States-India Nuclear Cooperation Approval and Nonproliferation Enhancement Act	N

Note: Important enactments listed in chronological order, based on data from Mayhew (2022). *HLOGA reforms included with 2006 New Direction document, but not as part of main agenda.

4.5 New Direction for America: Summary

The Democrats' 2006 agenda may have been "less ambitious and more informal" than the 1994 Republican Contract with America, as *CQ Weekly* noted,[118] but the New Direction for America emerged from similar minority-party impulses and had the same kind of mixed impact on legislating after the election. Democrats negotiated a concise messaging agenda that excluded many elements that would be internally controversial or publicly polarizing, choosing instead an agenda that tacked toward the priorities of their more vulnerable incumbents. The minority-party leadership used speeches and floor motions to highlight these issues in 2005–06, and the party's more ideological and safer incumbents tended to publicize the agenda more once it was unveiled during the campaign.

---

[118] "Manifesto for the First 100 Hours."

The agenda's mark could be seen in overall legislative issue priorities, which shifted toward New Direction topics in roll calls and committee work, and specific action on the agenda drove major work in the House during the first session of the new Congress, with about nine items eventually enacted into law that connected explicitly to New Direction promises. Those measures, in turn, shaped the initial important enactments of the 110th Congress, though the Democrats soon ran out of political opportunities and faced a rapidly changing national issue agenda.

5 Conclusions and Implications

Congressional election agendas have become a common part of the American political landscape, particularly for the party out of power in midterm elections. It has been easy to doubt the importance of these efforts since there is no evidence that even the most prominent agendas have directly reshaped what voters do. But there is evidence that they shape what Congress does. The 2006 New Direction for America and the 1994 Contract with America each show how these mini-platforms can substantially affect congressional action and representation. Viewed from early development through postelection legislative activity, these cases come into focus: they look at first glance like familiar messaging politics, but selective and strategic messaging took the form of concrete promises, which in turn drove uneven but consequential policymaking attempts for party leadership after winning House majorities.

Both the Contract and the New Direction originated in House party leadership initiatives, and each party's leadership felt compelled to use a participatory process to decide on their agenda's content and to seek buy-in from the House rank and file. In each case, the leadership chose early on to limit the scope of the agenda, and both process evidence and the final agenda content show how the parties selected issue positions strategically. Targeting a conservative-leaning electorate, particularly in southern and western districts that represented opportunity for the GOP, Republicans in 1994 assembled a set of promises that aligned with the issue priorities of more conservative members of their conference. Democrats in 2006 offered pledges on issues of importance to their more vulnerable members, reflecting the party's need to build a majority on districts that were not deep blue. The chosen issues in each agenda were not new ones, as the leadership in each minority party had emphasized these priorities in messaging with motions to recommit, and the parties had attended to the topics disproportionately in their floor speeches. Once an agenda was announced (in the 2006 case), safer and more ideological incumbents were more likely to advertise it to their constituents.

After the new majorities took control in 1995 and 2007, the House leadership focused intently on their agenda promises. These priorities are clear in the aggregate activity of the House. In both instances, the new Congress paid significantly more legislative attention to the agenda issues in committee hearings and in floor voting. At the level of individual promises and legislative measures, leaders passed legislation in the House on nearly all agenda items in these two cases. The record thereafter in the legislative process is more mixed, but the parties could claim that at least some legislation was enacted in the majority of the agenda issue areas. Neither agenda dominated the entire Congress, and the majority of important enactments in both Congresses were off-agenda items. However, the election agendas mapped directly onto the first several major enactments in both the 104th and 110th Congresses. And the fading effects of the agendas are detectable in the second Congresses after the two agenda-focused elections, as some heightened attention continued, particularly in committee activity, and few important agenda-related enactments appear in the second Congress as well.

The Contract and New Direction cases are not representative of the range of congressional election agendas put forward since 1980. They represent one end of the spectrum, a kind of upper bound for organized, participatory agenda formation and for subsequent legislative follow through. Thinking back to the other examples discussed in Section 2, the 1994 and 2006 cases have the closest parallels with the midterm, minority-party example of Republicans in 2010. The GOP agenda in that year represented a long-term development effort as well as some follow-on attention after the party took the majority. When parties have promulgated election agendas in other contexts, the results have looked different. The 1996 Democratic agenda wound up having some influence on the broader party messaging in that presidential year, but Democrats remained in the congressional minority after the election. And a majority-party agenda, like the Democrats' in 1982, presaged little postelection policy with party control unchanged, but the agenda did advance a continuing conversation about the party's direction in the Reagan era. In short, not all congressional election agendas have played the same role, and the findings here highlight patterns of origins and outcomes for circumstances like 1994 and 2006. Future research should further consider the other purposes that agendas have served in majority party and/or presidential year cases, as well as the decisions to avoid agendas entirely in some years.

At least in the "upper bound" cases of 1994 and 2006, we see the outlines of a national, party-government campaign model – but in the complicated (and complicating) context of American bicameralism and separation of powers.[119] While district-level representation is and will remain important in a single-member district system, the Contract with America and the New Direction for America each offered promissory representation at the level of the congressional party, and party leaders in each case took seriously the resulting obligation to act on the agenda items they had advanced. The implications of this are several. First, at least for periods of time, we may see congressional promise-making and promise-keeping happening at multiple levels. The individual-level policy responsiveness that Sulkin (2005, 2011) has documented is joined in these cases with party-level responsiveness to promises, as party leaders behave as if they will be held accountable for the set of issue commitments they made. Second, particularly with a few prominent examples like 1994 and 2006 in the rearview mirror, party leaders may perceive an incentive to make agendas in order to enjoy governing benefits of agenda focus and mandate claims in the Congress after the expected gain of majority control.

But then a third implication is that this representational dynamic may set expectations for responsible party government – in the House caucus and/or in the public – that cannot fully be met. Curry and Lee (2020, 35–39) have shown that majority-party priorities are still most often achieved only in part, and only with substantial minority-party support. The analysis of legislative outcomes supports that claim with regard to election-focused agendas. And the findings about the Republican Conference's post-Contract search for direction highlight the further constraints on congressional majorities that come from their own coalition. Any narrow, selective set of issues that dominates legislating for a period of time is going to leave the party with pent-up demand from supporting groups for action on other important priorities that may be less easily addressed.

In his trenchant early assessment of the Contract with America, Richard Fenno (1997) saw reason to see these problems as inherent in strategic congressional election agendas themselves. Republicans, Fenno argued, "decided to take the document they had crafted for *electioneering* purposes . . . and adopt it wholesale as their *legislative* agenda." In doing so, however, "they deprived themselves of a chance to think about their legislative agenda in terms of trade-offs, or to make distinctions between what they would *like* to get and what they *had* to get." This approach left Republicans with success as measured by House passage, but it missed what was necessary

---

[119] Abramowitz (2013) has tentatively suggested that moving the American system in the direction of more party-government dynamics might be the best way to cope with polarization-enhanced policy gridlock.

for long-term governing: "Not only had they not understood the difference between passing the Contract and governing the country, but what was worse, they had mistaken one for the other" (Fenno 1997, 20–22).

In this view, the legislative responsiveness of 1995 and 2007 could begin to look more like continued messaging. Strategic messages define the minority party's national campaign agenda, which then drive passage of message bills for the new majority – maybe "it's messaging all the way down?" That view, though, would overlook the fact that Republicans in the 1990s and Democrats in the 2000s could claim credit for enacting some important agenda legislation. More broadly, we know that messaging legislation connects to governing outcomes in the long run, as congressional majorities seek unified government and eventually convert at least some message bills into policy (Gelman 2020). On balance, congressional election agendas invite expectations for party government that cannot be easily or quickly satisfied, and the party-desired outcomes that are achieved in the near term are limited and involve compromise. From the party's perspective, both successful and unsuccessful action has some longer-term benefit as the polarized parties sustain an ongoing pursuit of majorities and unified government.

Appendix

Contract with America Topic Coding, 104th Congress

Agenda category	Bill	Topic code	Subtopic code
Congressional reform	HR 1	20	2011
Term limits	HJ Res 73	20	2011
Fiscal responsibility	HR 2	20	2011
National security	HR 7	16	1600
Jobs/wages/regulations	HR 5	20	2001
	HR 830	20	2002
	HR 926	20	2002
	HR 1022	20	2002
	HR 925	2	200
	HR 1215	1	107
Legal reform	HR 956	15	1525
	HR 988	12	1210
	HR 1058	15	1502
Welfare	HR 4	13	1300
Tax cuts	HR 1215	1	107
Crime	HR 665	12	1200
	HR 666	12	1204
	HR 667	12	1210
	HR 668	9	900
	HR 728	20	2001
Social security/seniors	HR 660	2	204
Families	HR 1240	12	1207
	HR 1271	2	208

New Direction for America Topic Coding

Agenda category	Sentence	Topic code	Subtopic code
Real security	1	16	1600
	2	16	1619
	3	16	1619
	4	16	1604
	5	16	1615
	6	16	1615
	7	16	1608
Prosperity	1	5	505
	2	1	107
Opportunity	1	1	107
	2	6	607
	3	6	601
Energy independence	1	8	806
	2	8	803
Affordable health care	1	3	335
	2	3	398
Retirement security & dignity	1	13	1303
	2	5	503
	3	5	503

References

Abramowitz, A. I. (2013). *The Polarized Public? Why American Government is so Dysfunctional*. Upper Saddle River: Pearson.

Abramowitz, A. I. (2018). *The Great Alignment: Race, Party Transformation, and the Rise of Donald Trump*. New Haven: Yale University Press.

Abramowitz, A. I. & Webster, S. (2016). "The Rise of Negative Partisanship and the Nationalization of U.S. Elections in the 21st Century." *Electoral Studies* 41(March):12–22.

Adler, E. S. & Wilkerson, J. D. (2012). *Congress and the Politics of Problem Solving*. Cambridge: Cambridge University Press.

Adler, E. S. & Wilkerson, J. D. (2019). "Congressional Bills Project: 1991–2010, NSF 00880066 and 00880061." www.comparativeagendas.net/us.

American Political Science Association. (1950). "Toward a More Responsible Two-Party System." *American Political Science Review* 44(3, Part 2):15–36.

Asmussen Mathew, N. & Kunz, M. (2017). "Recruiting, Grooming, and Reaping the Rewards: The Case of GOPAC in the 1992 Congressional Elections." *Congress & the Presidency* 44(1):77–101.

Azari, J. R. (2014). *Delivering the People's Message: The Changing Politics of the Presidential Mandate*. Ithaca: Cornell University Press.

Bader, J. B. (1996). *Taking the Initiative: Leadership Agendas in Congress and the "Contract with America."* Washington, DC: Georgetown University Press.

Bara, J. (2005). "A Question of Trust: Implementing Party Manifestos." *Parliamentary Affairs* 58(3):585–599.

Bendavid, N. (2007). *The Thumpin': How Rahm Emanuel and the Democrats Learned to be Ruthless and Ended the Republican Revolution*. New York: Doubleday.

Bonilla, T. (2022). *The Importance of Campaign Promises*. Cambridge: Cambridge University Press.

Borghetto, E. & Belchior, A. M. (2020). "Party Manifestos, Opposition and Media as Determinants of the Cabinet Agenda." *Political Studies* 68(1):37–53.

Brandt, K. G. (2007). "The Ideological Origins of the New Democrat Movement." *Louisiana History: The Journal of the Louisiana Historical Association* 48(July):273–294.

Brouard, S., Grossman, E., Guinaudeau, I., Persico, S., & Froio, C. (2018). "Do Party Manifestos Matter in Policy-Making? Capacities, Incentives and Outcomes of Electoral Programmes in France." *Political Studies* 66(4):903–921.

Caillaud, B. & Tirole, J. (1999). "Party Governance and Ideological Bias." *European Economic Review* 43(4–6):779–789.

Childs, S. & Krook, M. L. (2009). "Analysing Women's Substantive Representation: From Critical Mass to Critical Actors." *Government and Opposition* 44(2):125–145.

Clark, J. H. (2017). "The Motion to Recommit in the US House." In J. R. Straus & M. E. Glassman, eds., *Party and Procedure in the United States Congress*, pp. 63–80, 2nd ed. Lanham: Rowman and Littlefield.

Continetti, M. (2022). *The Right: The Hundred Year War for American Conservatism*. New York: Basic Books.

Cox, G. W. & McCubbins, M. D. (2005). *Setting the Agenda: Responsible Party Government in the U.S. House of Representatives*. Cambridge: Cambridge University Press.

Crespin, M. H. & Rohde, D. (2022). "Political Institutions and Public Choice Roll-Call Database." https://ou.edu/carlalbertcenter/research/pipc-votes/.

Curry, J. M. & Lee, F. E. (2020). *The Limits of Party: Congress and Lawmaking in a Polarized Era*. Chicago: University of Chicago Press.

Ellis, C. & Stimson, J. (2012). *Ideology in America*. Cambridge: Cambridge University Press.

Fagan, E. J. (2018). "Marching Orders? U.S. Party Platforms and Legislative Agenda Setting 1948–2014." *Political Research Quarterly* 71(4):949–959.

Fagan, E. J. (2021). "Issue Ownership and the Priorities of Party Elites in the United States, 2004–2016." *Party Politics* 27(1):149–160.

Fenno, R. F., Jr. (1997). *Learning to Govern: An Institutional View of the 104th Congress*. Washington, DC: Brookings Institution Press.

Froio, C., Bevan, S., & Jennings, W. (2017). "Party Mandates and the Politics of Attention: Party Platforms, Public Priorities and the Policy Agenda in Britain." *Party Politics* 23(6):692–703.

Galvin, D. J. (2010). *Presidential Party Building: Dwight D. Eisenhower to George W. Bush*. Princeton: Princeton University Press.

Gelman, J. (2020). *Losing to Win: Why Congressional Majorities Play Politics Instead of Make Laws*. Ann Arbor: University of Michigan Press.

Gimpel, J. G. (1996). *Fulfilling the Contract: The First 100 Days*. Boston: Allyn and Bacon.

Green, M. N. (2015). *Underdog Politics*. New Haven: Yale University Press.

Green, M. N. & Crouch, J. (2022). *Newt Gingrich: The Rise and Fall of a Party Entrepreneur*. Lawrence: University Press of Kansas.

Greene, Z. & O'Brien, D. Z. (2016). "Diverse Parties, Diverse Agendas: Female Politicians and the Parliamentary Party's Role in Platform Formation." *European Journal of Political Research* 55(3):435–453.

Grossmann, M. & Hopkins, D. A. (2016). *Asymmetric Politics: Ideological Republicans and Group Interest Democrats*. New York: Oxford University Press.

Gulati, G. J. (2004). "Members of Congress and Presentation of Self on the World Wide Web." *Harvard International Journal of Press/Politics* 9(1):22–40.

Harbridge, L. (2015). *Is Bipartisanship Dead? Policy Agreement and Agenda-Setting in the House of Representatives*. Cambridge: Cambridge University Press.

Harmel, R. (2018). "The How's and Why's of Party Manifestos: Some Guidance for a Cross-National Research Agenda." *Party Politics* 24(3):229–239.

Harmel, R., Tan, A. C., Janda, K., & Smith, J. M. (2018). "Manifestos and the Two Faces of Parties: Addressing Both Members and Voters with One Document." *Party Politics* 24(3):278–288.

Harris, D. B. (2005). "Orchestrating Party Talk: A Party-Based View of One-Minute Speeches in the House of Representatives." *Legislative Studies Quarterly* 30(1):127–141.

Harris, D. B. (2013). "Let's Play Hardball: Congressional Partisanship in the Television Era." In S. A. Frisch & S. Q. Kelly, eds., *Politics to the Extreme: American Political Institutions in the Twenty First Century*, pp. 93–115. London: Palgrave Macmillan.

Harris, D. B. (2019). "Anticipating the Revolution: Michel and Republican Congressional Reform Efforts." In F. H. Mackaman & S. Q. Kelly, eds., *Robert H. Michel: Leading the Republican House Minority*, pp. 186–215. Lawrence: University Press of Kansas.

Heberlig, E. S. & Larson, B. A. (2012). *Congressional Parties, Institutional Ambition, and the Financing of Majority Control*. Ann Arbor: University of Michigan Press.

Heersink, B. (2018). "Party Brands and the Democratic and Republican National Committees, 1952–1976." *Studies in American Political Development* 32(1):79–102.

Hopkins, D. A. (2017). *Red Fighting Blue: How Geography and Electoral Rules Polarize American Politics*. Cambridge: Cambridge University Press.

Hopkins, D. J. (2018). *The Increasingly United States: How and Why American Political Behavior Nationalized*. Chicago: University of Chicago Press.

Hughes, T. (2018). "Assessing Minority Party Influence on Partisan Issue Attention in the US House of Representatives, 1989–2012." *Party Politics* 24(2):197–208.

Hughes, T. & Koger, G. (2022). "Party Messaging in the U.S. House of Representatives." *Political Research Quarterly* 75(3): 829–845. https://doi.org/10.1177/10659129211029712.

Jacobson, G. C. (1996). "The 1994 House Elections in Perspective." *Political Science Quarterly* 111(2):203–223.

Jacobson, G. C. (2015). "It's Nothing Personal: The Decline of the Incumbency Advantage in US House Elections." *Journal of Politics* 77:861–873.

Jones, D. R. (2015). "Partisan Polarization and the Effect of Congressional Performance Evaluations on Party Brands and American Elections." *Political Research Quarterly* 68(4):785–801.

Kabaservice, G. (2012). *Rule and Ruin: The Downfall of Moderation and the Destruction of the Republican Party.* New York: Oxford University Press.

Kittilson, M. C. (2010). "Women, Parties, and Platforms in Postindustrial Democracies." *Party Politics* 17(1):66–92.

Klinkner, P. A. (1994). *The Losing Parties: Out-Party National Committees, 1956–1993.* New Haven: Yale University Press.

Koopman, D. L. (1996). *Hostile Takeover: The House Republican Party, 1980–1995.* Lanham: Rowman and Littlefield.

Lee, F. E. (2009). *Beyond Ideology: Politics, Principles, and Partisanship in the US Senate.* Chicago: University of Chicago Press.

Lee, F. E. (2016). *Insecure Majorities: Congress and the Perpetual Campaign.* Chicago: University of Chicago Press.

Lee, F. E. (2017). "Legislative Parties in an Era of Alternating Majorities." In A. S. Gerber & E. Schickler, eds., *Governing in a Polarized Age: Elections, Parties, and Political Representation in America*, pp. 115–142. Cambridge: Cambridge University Press.

Lynch, M. S. (2011). "The Motion to Recommit in the House of Representatives: Effects and Recent Trends." CRS Report for Congress RL34757.

Mansbridge, J. (2003). "Rethinking Representation." *American Political Science Review* 97(4):515–528.

Mayhew, D. R. (1974). *Congress: The Electoral Connection.* New Haven: Yale University Press.

Mayhew, D. R. (2005). *Divided We Govern: Party Control, Lawmaking, and Investigations, 1946–2002.* New Haven: Yale University Press.

Mayhew, D. R. (2022). "Datasets and Materials: Divided We Govern." https://campuspress.yale.edu/davidmayhew/datasets-divided-we-govern/.

Meinke, S. R. (2016). *Leadership Organizations in the House of Representatives: Party Participation and Partisan Politics.* Ann Arbor: University of Michigan Press.

Pearson, K. & Dancey, L. (2011). "Elevating Women's Voices in Congress: Speech Participation in the House of Representatives." *Political Research Quarterly* 64(4):910–923.

Peters, R. M., Jr. & Rosenthal, C. S. (2010). *Speaker Nancy Pelosi and the New American Politics*. New York: Oxford University Press.

Peterson, D. A. M., Grossback, L. J., Stimson, J. A., & Gangl, A. (2003). "Congressional Response to Mandate Elections." *American Journal of Political Science* 47(3):411–426.

Philpot, T. S. (2007). *Race, Republicans, and the Return of the Party of Lincoln*. Ann Arbor: University of Michigan Press.

Policy Agendas Project. (2019). "The Policy Agendas Project at University of Texas at Austin." www.comparativeagendas.net/us.

Procopio, C. H. (1999). *A Brave Newt World? Republican Campaign Strategies in the 1994 Congressional Elections*. PhD Thesis. Indiana University.

Rae, N. C. (1998). *Conservative Reformers: The Freshman Republicans in the 104th Congress*. Armonk: M. E. Sharpe.

Rae, N. C. & Campbell, C. C. (1999). "From Revolution to Evolution: Congress under Republican Control." In N. C. Rae & C. C. Campbell, eds., *New Majority or Old Minority: The Impact of Republicans in Congress*, pp.1–17. Lanham: Rowman and Littlefield.

Ranney, A. (1954). *The Doctrine of Responsible Party Government: Its Origins and Present State*. Urbana: University of Illinois Press.

Reinhard, D. W. (1983). *The Republican Right since 1945*. Lexington: University Press of Kentucky.

Roberts, J. M. (2005). "Minority Rights and Majority Power: Conditional Party Government and the Motion to Recommit in the House." *Legislative Studies Quarterly* 30(2):219-234.

Rohde, D. W. (1991). *Parties and Leaders in the Postreform House*. New Chicago: University of Chicago Press.

Rosenbluth, F. M. & Shapiro, I. (2018). *Responsible Parties: Saving Democracy from Itself*. New Haven: Yale University Press.

Royed, T. J., Baldwin, J. N., & Borrelli, S. A. (2019). "The United States." In E. Naurin, T. J. Royed, & R. Thomson, eds., *Party Mandates and Democracy: Making, Breaking, and Keeping Elections Pledges in Twelve Countries*, 101–121. Ann Arbor: University of Michigan Press.

Russell, A. (2021). *Tweeting is Leading: How Senators Communicate and Represent in the Age of Twitter*. New York: Oxford University Press.

Russell, A. & Wen, J. (2021). "From Rhetoric to Record: Linking Tweets to Legislative Agendas in Congress." *Journal of Legislative Studies* 27(4):608–620.

Shogan, C. J. & Glassman, M. E. (2017). "Longitudinal Analysis of One-Minute Speeches in the House of Representatives." In J. R. Straus & M. E. Glassman, eds., *Party and Procedure in the United States Congress*, pp. 131–149, 2nd ed. Lanham: Rowman and Littlefield.

Sinclair, B. (1995). *Legislators, Leaders, and Lawmaking: The US House of Representatives in the Postreform Era*. Baltimore: Johns Hopkins University Press.

Sinclair, B. (2008). "Leading the New Majorities." *PS: Political Science and Politics* 41(1):89–93.

Smith, S. S. (2007). *Party Influence in Congress*. Cambridge: Cambridge University Press.

Somer-Topcu, Z., Tavits, M., & Baumann, M. (2020). "Does Party Rhetoric Affect Voter Perceptions of Party Positions." *Electoral Studies* 65(June):102–153.

Stewart, C. P. & Jenkins, J. A. (2013). *Fighting for the Speakership: The House and the Rise of Party Government*. Princeton: Princeton University Press.

Stid, D. (1996). "Transformational Leadership in Congress?" Paper prepared for presentation at the 1996 American Political Science Association Annual Meeting.

Strahan, R. (2007). *Leading Representatives: The Agency of Leaders in the Politics of the US House*. Baltimore: Johns Hopkins University Press.

Sulkin, T. (2005). *Issue Politics in Congress*. Cambridge: Cambridge University Press.

Sulkin, T. (2011). *The Legislative Legacy of Congressional Campaigns*. Cambridge: Cambridge University Press.

Sulkin, T. & Schmitt, C. (2014). "Partisan Polarization and Legislators' Agendas." *Polity* 46(3):430–448.

Theriault, S. M. (2015). "Party Warriors: The Ugly Side of Party Polarization in Congress." In J. A. Thurber & A. Yoshinaka, eds., *American Gridlock: The Sources, Character, and Impact of Political Polarization*, pp. 152–170. Cambridge: Cambridge University Press.

Victor, J. N. & Reinhardt, J. Y. (2018). "Competing for the Platform: How Organized Interests Affect Party Positioning in the United States." *Party Politics* 24(3):265–277.

Zelizer, J. E. (2020). *Burning Down the House: Newt Gingrich, the Fall of a Speaker, and the Rise of the New Republican Party*. New York: Penguin.

Acknowledgments

I thank Solomon Wise for excellent research assistance. Blynne Olivieri Parker and Michael Camp in Special Collections at University of West Georgia provided valuable guidance with the voluminous Newt Gingrich Congressional Papers, and Nathan Gerth assisted me with various congressional archives at the Carl Albert Center. I am grateful to Matt Green, Michael James, Danielle Lemi, Vivien Leung, and Christina Xydias for comments on this research, and to Cambridge Elements American Politics series editor Frances Lee for helpful suggestions and questions. I thank Tyler Hughes for sharing data used in the analysis. I thank the Bucknell Faculty Development Committee and the Carl Albert Center at the University of Oklahoma for financial support.

Cambridge Elements ≡

American Politics

Frances E. Lee
Princeton University

Frances E. Lee is Professor of Politics at the Woodrow Wilson School of Princeton University. She is author of *Insecure Majorities: Congress and the Perpetual Campaign* (2016), *Beyond Ideology: Politics, Principles and Partisanship in the U.S. Senate* (2009), and coauthor of *Sizing Up the Senate: The Unequal Consequences of Equal Representation* (1999).

Advisory Board

About the Series

The Cambridge Elements Series in *American Politics* publishes authoritative contributions on American politics. Emphasizing works that address big, topical questions within the American political landscape, the series is open to all branches of the subfield and actively welcomes works that bridge subject domains. It publishes both original new research on topics likely to be of interest to a broad audience and state-of-the-art synthesis and reconsideration pieces that address salient questions and incorporate new data and cases to inform arguments.

Cambridge Elements ☰

American Politics

Elements in the Series

A full series listing is available at: www.cambridge.org/core/series/elements-in-american-politics

Printed in the United States
by Baker & Taylor Publisher Services